ALFRED

The Passionate Life of
Alfred de Musset

CHARLOTTE HALDANE

D1393955

ANTHONY BLOND

First published 1960
by
Anthony Blond Ltd.
34 Beech Street, London, E.C.1

To Elizabeth Shalit

This book has been set in Baskerville type
face. It has been printed in Great Britain on
Antique Wove paper by Taylor Garnett
Evans & Co. Ltd., Watford, Herts, and
bound by them

CONTENTS

꒦꒦꒦꒦꒦꒦꒦꒦꒦꒦꒦꒦꒷꒷꒷꒷꒷꒷꒷꒷꒷꒷

ILLUSTRATIONS

ILLUSTRATIONS

Introduction

I

THE GREAT lover—the man who is irresistibly attractive to women because he himself finds them so—is a type that has nearly ceased to exist in our unromantic society. He has become an almost mythical figure incarnated chiefly in certain film-stars, a symbol of the wishful thinking of millions of love-hungry men and women.

George Sand was the arch-type of the *femme fatale*. Among her galaxy of lovers, however, only two were men of genius, Alfred de Musset and Frédéric Chopin. Yet her later liaison with the Polish composer was not nearly so dramatic nor so passionate as her affair with Alfred, one of the most extra-ordinary in all life and literature.

Merely to tell the story of 'the lovers of Venice', as they have been called, would be to give an unfairly lop-sided picture of Alfred de Musset, who was only twenty-three when he fell under George's spell, from which to the end of his life, at forty-seven, he never wholly freed himself.

His sufferings inspired his poems, which include some of the greatest in the French language. He also wrote an auto-biographical novel, *La Confession d'un Enfant du Siècle*, sixteen plays and *Proverbes*, several of which have become classics, many short stories and tales and a great deal of criticism which was published in the press of his day.

In *La Confession d'un Enfant du Siècle* Alfred de Musset deliberately set out to express the sense of frustration of a debilitated post-war generation. The novel, written in the first person singular, was a passionate protest against the aftermath of war.

It was only late in his life that Alfred de Musset received his

7

rightful recognition as a great dramatist. Ever since the first production at the Comédie-Française of *Un Caprice* in 1847 his plays have had an unbroken success there and recently also on television, for which their gay and concise plots, simple sets and few characters make them eminently suitable.

2

This biography does not attempt to deal critically or comprehensively with all Musset's works. It is simply the story of 'The Child of the Century', of the man, the lover, and—since in his case the two are almost synonymous—the poet. I have given only brief summaries of those of his writings that have autobiographical significance. These do, however, include nearly all his greatest poems.

It is perhaps the biographer's most difficult task to present a poet to a foreign public. Those of Musset's great contemporaries who wrote prose—the novelists Stendhal and Balzac, for instance—have become known in translation to millions of readers all over the world. The same is true of the musical geniuses of his time—Rossini, Berlioz, Chopin—and the painters such as Ingres and Delacroix. To do justice to a poet it is necessary to attempt to translate at least some of his most important lyrics or passages from them and in no case more so than in Alfred de Musset's, since most of his greatest verse was inspired by his suffering heart. Unfortunately the language barrier is in a few cases insuperable. The last four lines of *Souvenir* are untranslatable because there is in English no worthy rhyme for 'God' and the poem's whole effect rests on the final word—*Dieu*. However the sweetness and power of Musset's genius is fully revealed in the original French versions that precede the translations.

3

I am sincerely grateful to those friends in Paris who so kindly helped me in my research into Alfred de Musset's life and works, especially to Monsieur and Madame Olivier de Grandcourt de Musset and Madame Ledru, granddaughter of Hermine de Musset, for much invaluable information and for allowing me to include hitherto unpublished photographs of some of the poet's drawings and cartoons. Madame E. Blondel-Flory showed me over George Sand's former 'attic' on the Quai Malaquais and Mademoiselle A. Leker over the apartment in the Rue du Mont-Thabor in which Alfred de Musset lived for ten years until his death there. I am also grateful to Monsieur Jean de Beer, to Monsieur Jean Pommier, and to Monsieur Jacques Suffel. I am deeply indebted to several librarians for great assistance, notably to Madame Sylvie Chevalley, head librarian of the Comédie-Française and her assistant Mademoiselle Geneviève Delune; to the staffs of the libraries of the Institut Français de Londres and the Kensington Borough Council, for the loan of several books. I owe a special word of thanks to Mademoiselle Madeleine Chabrier, conservateur at the Bibliothèque Nationale, for her great help in collecting the photographs of portraits, drawings and cartoons.

⇒⇒⇒ I ⇐⇐⇐

Life's delicate child

I

'OH, HURRY up, *Maman*, please, or my new red shoes will be old!' Alfred, aged three, was dancing up and down with impatience whilst his adoring mother combed out his long golden ringlets.

Those famous first words of his would hardly seem worthy of quotation had they been uttered by some ordinary little boy anxious to show off his new red shoes. But even at three, Alfred de Musset was no ordinary little boy. He was an exceptionally beautiful child, already restless, impatient to enjoy life to the full, who was to become France's greatest lyric poet, gayest dramatist, and most romantic lover.

He was born in Paris on 11 December 1810, when Napoleon was at the height of his power, which, however, was soon to wane. A new generation of young men, to which Alfred belonged, was to find no military glories such as their fathers had known as an outlet for their romantic dreams. Many of them grew to manhood psychologically unstable, groping and hoping for some certainty, some happiness, that seemed forever out of reach. Alfred de Musset was destined to become both the embodiment and the mouthpiece of his angry, frustrated generation, *L'Enfant du Siècle*.

Even as a very young child he seemed to know that he had been born to love and be loved more passionately than most of his romantic contemporaries, but that love was to be the source of his inspiration only through suffering. The pattern of his whole life was set in his earliest years: a constant alternation between exaltation and despair, a futile struggle to bridge the gap between his own visionary world and harsh reality.

The Mussets belonged to an old and distinguished family.

In 1580 one of their ancestors, Guillaume Musset, had married
the daughter of Cassandra Salviati, who bore the name of one
of the great Florentine families of the Renaissance and who
herself had been the beloved of the great French poet Ronsard,
who, with Joachim du Bellay had founded the group of poets
known as the Pleïades. Alfred's great-grandmother bore the
name of this latter poet. A great-aunt was a descendant of the
family of Joan of Arc.

Alfred's father, Victor-Donatien de Musset-Pathay, was
a man of culture and ability. He had fought in the great
Napoleonic campaigns. In his novel, *La Confession d'un
Enfant du Siècle*, Alfred de Musset described his own generation
and his father's in a passage which has become one of the
most famous in French literature:

> Conceived between two battles, going to school to the
> sound of beating drums, thousands of children, as they
> attempted to develop their youthful muscles, looked at one
> another with sombre eyes. From time to time their wounded
> fathers would appear, lift them on to the shoulders of their
> gold-braided uniforms, then put them down again and
> remount their steeds.
>
> One man alone was then the life of Europe; the remain-
> ing human beings attempted to fill their lungs with the
> air he had breathed. . . .
>
> Never were there so many sleepless nights as in the
> days of that man . . . never did greater silence reign than
> around those who spoke of death. Nor was there ever
> greater joy, more life, more resounding of trumpets of war
> in all hearts; never were suns brighter than those that
> dried all that blood. . . .

Alfred and his brother Paul grew up worshipping Napoleon,
who had brought France so much glory and so much suffering.
Their father embodied that glory for them and even as small
boys they were preparing to follow in his footsteps. But the
Napoleonic saga petered out in the desolation of Saint Helena.
For the sons of his warriors no comparable military glamour
lay ahead. Yet the Mussets, like many of their generation,

remained loyal and fervent Bonapartists. Even after the Emperor's downfall, Paul and Alfred continued to believe that one day he would return to lead them, as he had led their father, to the conquest of Europe.

It was very early in his boyhood, as his dream gradually faded, that Alfred felt a sense of frustration, a lack of enthusiasm for the age into which he himself had been born, deprived of the chance of a romantic military career.

Victor de Musset possessed considerable originality and wit. Although in later years a civil servant, holding a post in the Ministry of War, he was completely unbureaucratic and held liberal political opinions. He had dabbled in literature and was an authority on Jean-Jacques Rousseau, of whom he wrote a biographical study which was very well received.

Alfred's maternal grandfather, Claude-Antoine Guyot-Desherbiers, was also a man of wit and erudition, a charming character. His uncle Desherbiers remained his life-long friend and admirer.

But apart from his mother, the most important person in Alfred's childhood and in some ways throughout his life was his elder brother Paul, born five years earlier. A great deal of Alfred's childish precocity and many of his weaknesses and faults were due to their mutual devotion. It was Paul who aided and abetted their mother in attempting to protect Alfred from any alarming emotional experience that might have encouraged him to face life more realistically, who first read to him and later with him, tales of romance and adventure that prematurely stimulated the smaller boy's too vivid imagination. Alfred was no different from many spoiled children in his determination always to gain his ends. But when he resorted to the usual childish methods to do so he met with no corrective discipline whatever. On one occasion, in a fit of hysterical frenzy, he smashed a mirror in the drawing-room, cut up some new curtains with a pair of scissors and ruined a large map of Europe by dripping red sealing-wax over it—all in one day. These three acts of childish vandalism went totally unpunished because, according to his brother, as soon as Alfred calmed down he was deeply contrite.

If the superstition that it is unlucky to break a mirror has any truth in it, this was certainly so in Alfred's case. For this lack of even the mildest discipline in early childhood inevitably had the effect of perpetuating his tendency to hysteria, to create a behaviour pattern he never outgrew—to make a dreadful scene and himself so ill in the doing of it that those who loved him, fearing for his health and sanity, invariably forgave him.

Alfred's fascination for his family was enhanced by his nearly irresistible charm and gaiety. Even as a small child he already dramatized his experiences and seems to have seen the world as a stage and men and women as players on it almost from infancy. When his mother had taken him to church for the first time he asked her, as they walked home: 'Shall we go again next Sunday to see this play called the Mass?'

In his young days it was customary to shut naughty little boys in a dark cupboard. Paul, when so punished, would bear it with silent pride. Not so Alfred, the future playwright of the Comédie-Française. When such mild correction had to be administered he was not afraid, either. On one such occasion moans were heard from the cupboard, followed by a heart-rending monologue:

'Oh, how unhappy I am! If I really deserve to be punished by my darling Mama, who loves me so much, I must have been very naughty. What can I do to make her forgive me? What a bad boy I am! I suppose it's God that's punishing me!'

As these dramatic self-accusations continued his mother, taken in by such pathetic repentance, soon let him out. Alfred's little act having succeeded, his mood instantly changed. 'You're not "tender-hearting" at all!' he reproached her angrily.

During his early childhood the family lived in an old mansion near the *hôtel* de Cluny. In one room in this house was a heavy ceiling rafter, of which Alfred had a claustrophobic dread. One day his aunt tried to take away from him a kitten he was holding and, as children will, half strangling. He finally surrendered the poor little beast to her but as he did so, said furiously:

'All right, here's your cat, take it. But it'll scratch you and tear your dress. The rafter'll fall down and crush you, and I shall go to dinner at Bagneux!'

Dinner at Bagneux, the country house of his great-aunt, was a regular Sunday treat to which Alfred looked forward, for he was even then passionately fond of the country. But this childish threat was the first recorded instance of the nightmarish anxiety which was to haunt him all his life. When in later years his brother tried to reason him out of one of his caprices or follies he would answer :

'I know, I know. The rafter will crash down on me, and you will go to dinner at Bagneux!'

In due course the boys were sent to school. In 1817, Paul became a boarder; Alfred, still too young, went as a day-boy. It was Paul who had to bear the brunt of the persecution the two young Bonapartists endured from their royalist school-fellows—pro-Bourbons to a man. Very fortunately for them Paul caught measles at school. Alfred followed suit and after the holidays their parents engaged a tutor to teach them at home. In 1819, Paul was sent to another boarding-school. Alfred, who was only nine, lived at home and went to the Lycée Henri IV. On his first day there another disaster befell him. His adoring mother had still not been able to bring herself to cut off his long golden curls and he was dressed in a 'Little Lord Fauntleroy' suit of black velvet with a lace collar. His schoolfellows not surprisingly received this new pupil with boos and jeers. He returned home in tears demanding that the golden locks be shorn immediately.

But this sacrifice did not appease his persecutors. Alfred was an exceptionally gifted scholar and was placed in a class with much older boys. Even so, he learned so easily that he almost invariably received top marks. He was already ambitious and the least failure affected him emotionally. At home his mother quickly comforted him but at school his successes made him even more unpopular with his less gifted but less spoiled and tougher classmates. That he was the smallest of them did not deter them from punishing him. During a whole month they lay in ambush for him every day and beat him up so unmercifully that he came home with torn clothes and a bloody nose, until a family friend, an older and stronger boy, dispersed Alfred's enemies with heavier blows than theirs.

Alfred's scholastic successes continued until the end of his schooldays. In his last year he read philosophy with, apparently,

B

remarkably mature understanding. The Mussets were Catholics. But Alfred was neither then nor ever in his life attracted by conventional religious worship. He tried with genuine humility to believe in God. But, as he wrote in his famous *Confession*, the youth of his day grew up in a state of disenchantment, of *désespérance* (hopelessness) 'as if humanity were in such a state of lethargy that those who searched for its pulse found it no longer beating'. Like that soldier who when asked of old, 'In what do you believe?' replied 'In myself,' so the youth of France when asked that question again, answered 'In nothing.'

Many years later he modified this nihilistic view when he wrote his magnificent poem, *Espoir en Dieu* which expressed, if not faith, the longing to believe.

2

On the threshold of puberty Alfred was outwardly a brilliant success. At school he won, as his proud mother wrote to a friend, 'cartloads of prizes' and was taken up by the most aristocratic of his classmates, the Duc de Chartres, son of the Duc d'Orléans. Another of his school friends, Paul Foucher, introduced him to the arch-priest of Romanticism, the poet Victor Hugo. In his house there were gatherings of all the leading literary men of the day, including Alfred de Vigny, a distinguished poet, Prosper Mérimée the novelist—author of *Carmen*—and Sainte-Beuve, the famous critic. At that time none of them paid much attention to the handsome, delightful, gay lad who was privileged to hear them recite their verses or plays to one another. For Alfred was no infant prodigy and his own poetic talent did not flower until some years later.

Meanwhile, the brothers spent most of their holidays at the country houses of their numerous relatives, for like most Parisians the Mussets had one foot in Paris and one on the land. Their favourite among these small estates was Cogners, which belonged to their great-uncle, the Marquis de Musset. But it became identified in Alfred's memory with near-tragedy. When he was fourteen he was allowed to take part in his first shoot there. He was given an old gun which was apparently defective, and as he followed Paul along a woodland path, carrying this gun under his arm, it suddenly and accidentally went off. The pellets buried themselves in the soil, only a few inches from Paul's right foot. When his brother turned round he saw that Alfred had almost fainted with horror at the thought that he might have wounded him. The shock was so great that he developed a temperature and for years afterwards referred to 1824 as 'the year in which I nearly killed my brother'.

In 1827 he was again spending his holidays at Cogners. He had now to decide on a profession. Which was it to be, law or medicine? Alfred's father was not pressing him to make up his mind; all he wanted was that his son should work hard at whichever career attracted him. But Alfred was neither then nor ever in his life attracted to a so-called regular profession, which would entail sitting at a desk in an office for a definite number of hours each day. At sixteen, apart from having scribbled a few unimportant verses he had shown no signs at all of literary genius, except, possibly, unusual facility. Yet he already had a sense of his vocation. The following passage describing his still undefined adolescent feelings is a prose-poem which reveals clearly how even as a boy he was susceptible to influences which have always profoundly moved poets, but few of their more humdrum fellow-men:

After love, my sole treasure was my freedom. Even at puberty I worshipped it almost savagely; I had, as it were, consecrated my heart to it. One day my father, who was already thinking of my future, suggested several careers to me, leaving me to choose between them. I was leaning against my window-sill, looking at a slim and solitary poplar tree, swaying in the garden. I was thinking about those various professions and trying to decide on one or the other. I turned them all over in my mind and then, feeling no interest in any of them, I let my thoughts wander. It seemed to me that I suddenly felt the earth moving and that my senses could apprehend the silent, invisible power that drew it through space; I saw it rise into the heavens; it seemed as if I were aboard a ship;

the poplar before my eyes was like a mast; I stood up, stretched out my arms and cried: 'It is little enough to be a passenger for a day on this ship floating in the ether; it is little enough to be a man, a mere dark spot on that ship; I will be a man, but never any particular kind of man!'

Although this was written when he was adult, even at seventeen the poetic temperament from which his great lyrical gifts were to spring was already established. Even then, also, Alfred was experiencing the restlessness, the sense of futility, the lack of spiritual and intellectual certainty which were to haunt him all his life and to escape which he increasingly sought release in stimulants and sedatives, in alcohol and drugs.

Living in the country alone with his great-uncle—Paul had returned to Paris—he was suffering the first pangs of that acute boredom which was the reverse of his passionate eagerness to experience and enjoy life to the full. He relieved his misery in a long letter to his friend Paul Foucher, an extraordinary piece of self-analysis for a boy of seventeen, as clear intellectually as it was confused emotionally. His devotion to his charming and cultured great-uncle was mingled with youthful impatience at the old gentleman's kind advice:

> You have read Shakespeare's *Hamlet* and you know the effect the wise and erudite Polonius had on him! . . . I am bored and sad but I haven't the courage to work, and what should I work at?

He would have liked to write but could not do so because he felt incapable of rising to his own ambitious standards:

> I would not want to write unless I could be either a Shakespeare or a Schiller, and so I do nothing! I feel that the worst that can happen to a man of strong passions is to have none. I am not in love; I do nothing . . . I would give away my life for two sous if, in order to leave it, one did not have to die.

It was fairly usual in the Romantic age for adolescents to suffer quite sincerely such literary melancholy. With that clear intelligence which was always at war with his emotions, even at seventeen, Alfred could answer himself in the words of his elders:

> All that is merely a matter of your age, my child. I was the same when I was young. You should have a little amusement, but not too much, and then you will study law and go into a lawyer's office. . . .

But Alfred would not accept this dusty answer. He was not in love, yet longed to love—'I need to love'. And—

> I have no courage even to think. If at this moment I were in Paris I would drown what little good there remains in me in punch and beer, and I would feel relieved. Sick people are put to sleep with opium, although their sleep will be deadly. I would do the same to my own self. . . .

Punch and beer. . . . He might have chosen this sordid mixture of alcoholic sedatives purely for literary effect, for the sake of contrast. But unfortunately there is no doubt that Alfred became an alcoholic at an age when most other boys taste liquor for the first time merely in order to enjoy a mild 'lift'. He found it abhorrent, would swallow it down at a draught as if it were bitter medicine, with no pleasure. Henceforth he drank to relieve the nervous tension which otherwise became too intolerable to be borne. In October he went to stay with another relative. His thoughts we still running on the same sombre lines; he must love and be loved. He was then beginning to think of himself as a poet, for he wrote in a further letter to Paul Foucher, 'in me poetry is the sister of love'. But this longing for love was curiously and prophetically blended with hatred:

> In theory I hate women, but I know, nevertheless, that I shall be caught.

And if the women he loved deceived him, were unfaithful to him, they would have no satisfaction from it; he would have expected such conduct in advance. Before ever being in love Alfred was preparing himself for the torments of jealousy he would feel as soon as this overwhelming experience befell him; the whole pattern of his future behaviour was predicted in this strange declaration. For him love was not to be synonymous with marriage or with mutual affection and understanding. It was to be a battle between him and the beloved who would torture and wound one another almost to death. His method of staunching his wounds would be to draw from them some of the greatest love poems ever written.

3

It would have been surprising had this highly emotional and introspective boy not felt repugnance at the thought of becoming a dry-as-dust lawyer. But it is even more surprising that Alfred decided on his return to Paris to study medicine. No one could have had less vocation for a profession demanding a realistic outlook and steady nerves than a romantic and budding poet preoccupied with the analysis of his own emotions and sensations, attracted passionately by all that was good and beautiful and irresistibly by their opposites, a slow but ineluctible descent into the world of drinking-booths and brothels. It was possibly the morbid side of his imagination that impelled him. Even as a small child his family had known that the least emotional shock was liable to upset his precarious mental balance. They could hardly therefore have been surprised at the speedy and disastrous termination of Alfred's medical studies. For as soon as he began his courses in anatomy and beheld the corpses laid out in the dissecting-room, he was overcome by such horror that he fled helter-skelter from the hospital. An acute attack of nerves followed and for years afterwards he would re-live this terrifying experience in nightmares from which he awoke screaming.

Hysteria is a psychopathic condition, but one with a purpose. No reasoned arguments on his part could have convinced his family more completely of his good intentions with regard to a working career and at the same time of the lack of robustness which would make it impossible for him to pursue one. For subconsciously Alfred knew exactly what he wanted and could not have more successfully set about attaining his ends. He would continue to be 'life's delicate child', the spoiled darling of his family and soon of some of the most elegant salons in Paris. He was growing into a delightfully handsome youth, to become almost irresistible to women. He was beginning to be a poet. And he had always had another minor talent which now proved useful. He could draw and illustrate charmingly. So he decided to study painting.

II

'What did I do with my youth?'

I

EUGÈNE DELACROIX, the famous French romantic painter of the first half of the nineteenth century, and one of Alfred's life-long friends, told George Sand: "Had he wished, he might have become a great artist."

Alfred's talent as a draughtsman undoubtedly justified this view. His drawings, and especially his caricatures and cartoons, were no less than brilliant. Like all great artists he had his own idiom, his style, and a caricature by Alfred de Musset is instantly recognizable. His observation was razor-sharp and unsparing, as much of himself as of his subjects, even the prettiest of the many women he loved and drew. He had an unusual lightness of touch; his sketches of children (such as George Sand's son and daughter, Maurice and Solange) are enchanting. The album of drawings depicting the courtship and marriage of the singer, Pauline Garcia, to Louis Viardot, each with its 'legend', proves that had he lived in our time Alfred de Musset could have earned a fortune as a strip-cartoonist. But he appears to have taken his own talent at the same valuation as his contemporaries, merely as an amusing parlour-trick with which to entertain himself and his friends.

Alfred may have given up any serious intention of becoming a painter for the same reason that at first inhibited his creative gifts as a poet and dramatist. If he were not to be a Schiller or a Shakespeare he would not wish to be a writer. He had a genuine passion for the great masters of painting, especially the Italians, and probably felt his talent to be too hopelessly inferior to them even to attempt to emulate them. In spite of his affectations of indifference to social opinion, Alfred was immensely ambitious. Feeling himself incapable of reaching the highest artistic standards he preferred not to paint at all. He studied only for six months, when he went regularly to the Louvre, to copy the masters there. And among the few of his own more serious efforts was a portrait of Byron.

Byron died in 1823, when Alfred was thirteen. His cult in France, among the romantic intellectuals in revolt against their own too rigid classicism and about to break with it, was of great importance in the lives of many of them. It was Byronism that largely attracted Franz Liszt, the prodigious young Hungarian pianist, to the Countess Marie d'Agoult; it was in a completely Byronic tradition that they eloped to Switzerland in 1835. Alfred was by no means unique in his adoration of Byron; he was so, however, in that he was to become in many ways Byron's French counterpart. Like Byron, he was strikingly good-looking and elegant, a youthful aristocrat and an aspiring dandy; his emotions never perhaps at this time wholly sincere, were constantly inflamed by his imagination; he was determined to empty the cup of life to the full, to enjoy and to suffer, to be loving and charming and also wicked, in the romantic sense of the term. Above all, he had a similar literary facility, could compose verses on any subject at any length, and like his model, was also to find himself famous on publishing his first poems at the age of nineteen. Unlike Byron—and this was the significant difference between them—Alfred de Musset was no man of action but intensely introspective—a poet, nothing but a poet, and wholly a poet throughout his life. In Alfred's poetry there was, as in Byron's, a constant interplay of light and shadow, of humour, gaiety, even cynicism, as well as lyricism and melancholy.

2

'Poetry is the sister of love.' In Alfred's later love affairs it was never quite clear where literature ended and love —genuine, sincere, uncomplicated—began. To him the woman he loved was a synonym for inspiration.

Paul recorded in his brother's biography that Alfred first fell in love at the age of four. This precocious emotion was aroused by the visit to his family of a charming young girl cousin from Liège. Alfred was sitting on the drawing-room sofa, playing with his toys. He got up, went over, and asked his mother who she was.

'Your cousin,' he was told, 'her name is Clélie.'

'Oh, she's mine, is she? Very well, I'll take her, and keep her.'

But to him she was not just another toy. He proposed to Clélie, who, naturally, 'accepted' him. When in due course she went home, Clélie told Alfred not to forget her.

'Forget you!' he exclaimed with dramatic seriousness. 'Don't you know that your name is inscribed on my heart with a pen-knife?'

This sort of childish emotion was not in the least exceptional. Small boys and girls constantly announce their intention of marrying their loved older relatives—mother, father, sister, cousin—when they grow up. But in this instance Alfred's family conspired once again to protect his infant sensitivity from all contact with reality, and went to fantastic lengths to do so. For when Clélie married, no one dared refer to this 'tragedy' in his presence, and their friends and callers, even, were warned not to do so. One day, nevertheless, someone tactlessly mentioned Madame Moulin—Clélie's married name.

'Whom are you talking about?' Alfred demanded suspiciously. 'Where is Madame Moulin?' Whereupon they actually led him up to a strange young lady who happened to be calling—no doubt with conspiratorial winks and nods—and 'Here she is,' they lied.

It was not until nearly ten years later, when Alfred was a schoolboy, that the news of his cousin's marriage was at last broken to him. Even then he took it badly, suspecting that Clélie had been merely making fun of him all this time, and unable to bear the disillusionment.

This episode, which, had it been treated by Alfred's family with the sense of proportion and triviality normally given to such childish affairs, might have left no lasting impression on him, was carefully remembered and even recounted in his biography by his loving but misguided brother Paul. Alfred himself certainly never forgot it. His affection for Clélie and hers for him endured to the end of their lives. In 1836—Alfred was then a young man of twenty-six—she and the Mussets fell out over some question of property rights. A legal case was pending when Alfred one day took a coach and went to visit Clélie, arriving unexpectedly. They embraced one another, and the financial differences were immediately settled.

The psychological harm done to him by the deception his family had practised on his infant mind was not so easily remedied. Indeed it may well have set the pattern for all his future amorous relationships. The 'betrayal' of Clélie's marriage, the lies and subterfuges with which it had been concealed from him, the shock when he finally discovered the truth, his jealousy and above all the wound to his *amour-propre* —the fear that his beloved had been making a fool of him during all those years—these set up a traumatic condition from which he was never to be free. The pattern was repeated when he was old enough to know better; not once, but several times. He was to make many women suffer cruelly for Clélie's alleged unfaithfulness.

His first adolescent attachment, at eighteen, was again to a woman much older than himself. She was a coquette and merely amused herself by a casual flirtation with the charming and attractive youth. But now sister poetry came to the aid of her wounded sister, love. In future Alfred would draw on all his love affairs for his literary material, and reproduce them in his verse, plays, or stories. Never again would he love innocently, without the creative artist's awareness that one day he would make copy from his experience.

In his play, *Il ne faut jurer de rien*, published in 1836, the youthful hero, Valentin, explains to his uncle why he is determined to remain single:

I was sixteen, I had just left school, when a lovely lady offered me her favours. How can one know at that age what is harmless and what is a sin? One evening I was sitting by my mistress's fireside; her husband was also there. The husband said that he was going out. At those words a glance from my beloved made my heart leap with joy: we would be alone! I turned round and saw the poor man putting on his gloves. They were a greenish suede, too large, with a hole in one thumb. As he stood in the middle of the room, dragging them on, an imperceptible smile

played around his wife's lips and drew a light shadow around
the two dimples in her cheeks. Only a lover's eyes see such
smiles, for they are more often felt than seen. That one
penetrated my heart and I swallowed it like a sorbet.
But by a strange freak of fate the memory of that delicious
moment is for ever linked in my mind with that of two big
red hands thrusting into greenish gloves; there was something sad and pitiful in the sight of those trustful hands and
I have never thought of it since without feeling that
feminine smile tickling the edges of my own lips and
without swearing that no woman on earth would ever
make me draw a pair of gloves like those on to my own
hands.

There is little doubt that the bitter-sweet, subtle flavour of
this passage, like most of Alfred's best lines, had an autobiographical origin. Throughout his life his happiness and
success in love were ineluctably shot through with feelings of
guilt and deep distrust of the women who aroused his passion.
Nor did he himself ever draw on a pair of those symbolic
matrimonial gloves.

3

The psychological conflicts these love affairs with women
of his own class invariably aroused in him found a more
venal sexual appeasement. There was always the love that
could be bought, though love was perhaps not the right term
for the satisfaction he thus sought and obtained. Bitterly and
cynically, with a sense of self-disgust such as he had first
revealed in his early letters to Paul Foucher, Alfred went in
search of sordid pleasures. Here, too, literature crept in, for
in his *Confession d'un Enfant du Siècle* he analysed in detail both his
addiction and the unhappiness that had driven him to it.
Although this famous novel was not written until 1835 the
following passage nevertheless applies to Alfred's profound
disillusionment at a much earlier age than twenty-five, and
his first experiences of this kind may well have occurred when
he was only seventeen or eighteen. The story is told in the first

person singular by its hero, whom he calls Octave. Very late one night this young man is sitting on a bench, in the street, outside the home of his unfaithful mistress:

One night, as I sat on that bench in a state of the deepest misery, a workman out late came tottering past. He was mumbling to himself, senseless words interspersed with exclamations of joy: then he burst into song. He was drunk. He finally fell on to a bench outside another house, facing me. There he rocked himself to and fro for a time, and then went heavily to sleep. . . .

In spite of myself, that man distracted me from my unhappiness . . . I could not leave that door, although not for an empire would I have knocked on it. After having paced around in every direction, I stopped without thinking in front of the sleeper.

'What a sleep!' I said to myself. 'This man is certainly not dreaming, although at this very moment his wife may be opening the door of their garret to a neighbour. He is in rags, his cheeks are sunken and his hands work-worn; he must be some unfortunate who does not even get enough bread every day. When he wakes up, a thousand troubles and tribulations may await him; but to-night he had an *écu* in his pocket, with which he went and bought what he needed to drown his sorrows. . . . Now his mistress could betray him, or his best friend sneak into his hovel like a thief; even I, myself, could shake him by the shoulder and yell murder at him, or tell him that his house is on fire, but he would simply turn on his other side and go to sleep again.'

'Yet I,' I continued, as I strode up and down the street, 'who have enough in my pocket to send him to sleep for a year, cannot sleep; but am so madly proud that I dare not enter a drinking-shop, not even having noticed that if those who do so are unhappy, those who come out are happy. Oh, God! to think that a bunch of grapes trodden underfoot is enough to blow away the blackest misery and to cut all those invisible threads that bad luck throws across our paths. We weep like women, we suffer like martyrs; in our anguish it seems as if the world had fallen

in over us, and we settle down in tears, like Adam and
Eve outside the gates of Paradise. Yet to close a wound wider
than the earth, all we have to do is to move a hand and
moisten our throats. . . . As this man sleeps so peacefully
on his bench, why should I not do the same on mine?'

And so he went, although it was so late, in search of a wine-
shop and after several attempts found one that was still
open. There, when he was sufficiently drunk to be able to
forget his unhappiness and to look around him, he noticed a
group of men who belonged to that ambiguous class, the vilest
of all, which possessed neither respectability nor wealth but
only the vices of those who did. As they argued over a game of
cards a young girl with them left the group and came over
to his table. She was pretty, well-dressed; only her voice, rough
and common, resembled those of her companions. Seeing him
so young, so unhappy, so dangerously drunk, she spoke to
him kindly, almost maternally, and offered to take him home.
Octave allowed her to do so and she spent the rest of the
night in his bed.

Next morning he was filled with such self-disgust that he
felt on the verge of suicide. For the prostitute with whom he
had slept had a strange and horrible resemblance to the
unfaithful woman he loved. Octave (who was Alfred himself)
had discovered the ineluctible fact, admirably expressed by
Graham Greene, that 'the act of lust and the act of love are
the same; it cannot be falsified like a sentiment'. Confronted
with this shattering reality, he was again and again to seek
oblivion from it in the same sedative, in alcoholism. For the
cure had worked. It was base, ignoble, but there was no
other. And in the end it destroyed him.

4

At eighteen, however, life cannot be all gloom, even for the
most romantic young poet. In the spring of 1828 Madame de
Musset had rented a small flat in a large house at Auteuil,
then an idyllic Parisian suburb. Alfred would leave early in
the morning for the atelier where he was studying painting,

and return in the early evening, walking home through the Bois de Boulogne, reading his favourite poet at this period, André Chénier, who had died on the guillotine in 1794. And inspired by him as well as by Byron, Alfred himself wrote more and more verse.

At home there were gay parties of young people of his own age, including several charming young girls. The little group organized amateur theatricals in which Alfred played a leading part. He had already begun to write dramatic sketches in verse.

He had also returned to the group of poets and critics to which Paul Foucher had introduced him, who were known as *Le Cénacle*.

The importance to him of the *Cénacle* lay in the contacts which it brought him, particularly with two of its members, Sainte-Beuve and Charles Nodier.

There was never any great sympathy between the young, flamboyant and often flippant Alfred de Musset and the *Cénacle's* high-priest, Victor Hugo, who took himself very seriously and dramatically. Although the young poets and writers of Alfred's generation could not achieve military glory like their fathers, they made their own battles. These were fought out on the cultural plane, but were not by any means peaceful on that account. Led by Victor Hugo, the *Cénacle* plunged into a violent war against the earlier, classical tradition. This reversal of the former canons, which had grown both rigid and sterile, culminated in the production of Hugo's drama, *Hernani*, at the Comédie-Française in 1830, when there was a riot on the first night and free-for-all fights on every subsequent night of the forty-five performances, which in consequence, became known in French literature as '*Les batailles d'Hernani*'. But there was a great difference between the dramatic romanticism of Hugo and the purely lyrical inspiration of Musset.

Sainte-Beuve was a minor poet, who became a major critic, the most influential Frenchman of letters of the first half of the nineteenth century. His literary acumen was backed by enormous scholarship and industry. He was short and dumpy in appearance, and although he became the lover of Madame Hugo, was unattractive to women. He was nevertheless attracted to them, and in general to youth and beauty. He was charmed by that high-spirited, gay, amusing boy, Alfred de Musset, who had suddenly blossomed into one of the most delightful young men of his generation. Having heard the senior members of the *Cénacle* recite their poems, Alfred one morning burst into Sainte-Beuve's home, and half-seriously, half-flippantly, informed him that he, too, was a poet. When Sainte-Beuve heard his verses, he was convinced that Alfred's claim was justified. He wrote, in fact, to a friend that 'there is amongst us a child of genius'. Before long the entire *Cénacle* shared Sainte-Beuve's opinion. But Alfred's sense of humour erupted into a poem which created a sensation amongst them. It was quite unlike anything anyone had ever written before. It was entitled *Ballade à la Lune*, but was no sentimental hymn to the planet the romantics so loved to apostrophize in melancholy stanzas. It was, in fact, a youthful parody on this theme, written in beautifully turned short, crisp lines, beginning:

> C'était dans la nuit brune
> Sur le clocher jauni
> La lune
> Comme un point sur un I.

and ending with the same lines. This image of the moon, seen over a church steeple rising into the sky, 'like a dot on an I' was regarded as amusing and daring, but also as rather shocking. It was, of course, a poetic conceit of striking observation and originality. But the earnest members of the *Cénacle* found it rather too flippant and Alfred soon found them not sufficiently amusing. Although he was at the same time writing masses of more serious verse, he was also seeking his social distractions in a very different world, where gay parties, racing and gambling played a much greater role than literature.

Alfred was enthusiastically taken up by a group of rich young men known as '*les dandies*', imitators of those young Englishmen who had followed the cult of Beau Brummel. They affected the very tall hats, tight-waisted blue frock coats with huge collars, ornamental waistcoats, drain-pipe trousers and frilled shirts which Brummel had made obligatory for

Paul and Alfred de Musset as children, by Dufau

Alfred de Musset in fancy dress, by Achille Dévéria (*circa* 1830)

young men of fashion. Alfred, never to be out-done in youthful high spirits, did the same. He ordered his clothes from their tailors, the most expensive in Paris. The Mussets were far from poor, but his personal income hardly ran to such high living. Nevertheless, when Paul tried to make him face up to the consequences of such extravagance, Alfred replied:

> I want to know everything and to experience everything, not just to hear about life at second-hand. I feel as if I had two separate identities; one of them acts, the other looks on. If the first one behaves stupidly, the second one will learn from him. Sooner or later, God willing, I will pay my tailor. I do gamble, but I am not a gambler, and when I've lost my money it teaches me a better lesson than all the lectures in the world.

Alfred's arguments were puerile and would not have held water for an instant with any less partisan admirer than Paul. He was a gambler, lost his money over and over again, and never learned his lesson. But even gambling fed his talent. Years later this weakness of his was to form the basis for the plot of his enchanting little comedy *Un Caprice*. Paul, reporting their conversation in retrospect knew this. When it took place Alfred was still only an adolescent, budding poet. But after the event Paul's faith in him was justified. To his staid, respectable brother Alfred's glamour was a source of unending thrills and excitement. No doubt on that and on many subsequent occasions he helped him to pay both his tailor and his gambling debts.

5

In this conversation mention was also made for the first time of Alfred's belief that he had a dual personality, one of which acted, whilst the other looked on. This belief was also partly sincere, partly literary. In early nineteenth-century romantic literature this myth was one of the most popular. Heinrich Heine called his shadow or second personality his *'Doppelgänger'*—the man who walked beside him, observing and frequently mocking his words and actions. In 1813, Chamisso, another contemporary, romantic poet, born in France but brought up in Germany and writing in German, had published a story called *Peter Schlemihl*, about a man who sold his shadow to the devil. Heine, who settled in Paris in 1831, was undoubtedly influenced by him. Whether or not Alfred consciously applied this mythical concept to himself, he certainly believed in it quite sincerely. In times of fever, delirium or hallucination, he actually saw this other self. In 1835, at the height of his poetic power, he described him in detail in his great poem *La Nuit de Décembre*:

> Du temps que j'étais écolier,
> Je restais un soir à veiller
> Dans notre salle solitaire.
> Devant ma table vint s'asseoir
> Un pauvre enfant vêtu de noir,
> Qui me ressemblait comme un frère.

> One day at school I stayed alone,
> Keeping a vigil of my own,
> In all the class-room not another.
> Then at my desk a boy sat down,
> Dressed in a black and shabby gown,
> Who looked as like me as a brother.

He used the same theme in a prose play, *Les Caprices de Marianne*. As in his *Confession*, he chose the name Octave for one of his leading characters, and that of Coelio for the other. But Octave and Coelio were in fact two facets of Alfred's own personality. The cold-blooded rational Octave and the tender lovable Coelio both love Marianne; Coelio, not Octave, is killed by an assassin hired by her jealous husband. In the last scene Octave and Marianne visit Coelio's tomb. Octave tells Marianne:

> 'I alone in the whole world knew him. . . . For me alone his silent life contained no mysteries. The long evenings we spent together were like a refreshing oasis in an arid desert . . . Coelio was the better part of my own self, and it has gone to heaven with him. He was a man of another

day; he knew pleasure, but preferred solitude; he knew that illusions were deceptive, and yet he preferred his own illusions to reality. The woman who would have loved him would have been happy.'

'And the woman who loved you'—Marianne asks Octave—'would she not be happy?'

'I cannot love'—Octave replies—'only Coelio could love. . . . He alone was capable of illimitable devotion; he alone would have given his life for the women he loved. . . . I am only a libertine without a heart; I have no respect for women; the love I inspire in them is the same as I feel myself—the momentary intoxication of a dream . . . good-bye, now, to love and friendship. My place on earth is empty.'

'But not in my heart, Octave'—Marianne replies. 'Why do you say: Good-bye to love?'

'I do not love you, Marianne. It was Coelio who loved you.'

If those lines were written from a poet's imagination they were nevertheless wholly autobiographical. Who can decide whether a man is or is not what he thinks he is? Whether Alfred was in fact half tender-hearted and adoring youth, half cynical and heartless libertine, is not the crux of the matter. This is that he saw himself as such and throughout his life acted up to his own belief in his dual personality.

Throughout 1828 and 1829 he was leading the kind of life to be expected of a youthful, irresistible Coelio-Octave. Coelio read and wrote, both prose and verse; Octave amused himself extravagantly in high and frivolous society. Paul's pride in this brilliant social butterfly is reflected in a passage which is almost like a verbal rendering of a Chopin valse:

In the salons of Paris he soon forgot his gaming losses. Whether it was that the balls made a great impression on him, or whether it was due to his interest in painting, the fact remains that he remembered in astonishing detail the order in which the women had been seated around the ballroom, the colours of their gowns, their ornaments and headdresses. Luxury filled him with a kind of intoxication.

Like a child he admired the sparkling lights, laces, jewels. To dance with a real marquise, who wore real diamonds, in a vast ballroom as bright as daylight, seemed to him the height of happiness.

... In Achille Dévéria's salon, where he was a constant visitor, Alfred de Musset waltzed alternately with two young girls of the same age, both extremely pretty and charming, one as *ingénue* as the other, and great friends. Still as much of a child as they were, he would talk to them delightfully about fashions, clothes, chiffons. He would tell each of them in turn how lovely and charming the other was. When next day the girls exchanged confidences, they were unable to discover which of them he really preferred.

It was not, however, Alfred's talent for painting that was stimulated by these dazzling visual impressions, but his poetic facility, his ability to turn out charming lyrics in praise of the women and girls whose grace and elegance he admired. Very soon, too, the youthful flirtations and harmless intrigues in which he indulged were to provide material for the gay and witty playlets he began to write.

One of these, *A quoi rêvent les jeunes filles*, a light-hearted rhymed trifle, was first published in 1833. It was not performed until 1926, when it was given at the Comédie-Française with music by Claude Debussy, and where it has since been performed nearly two hundred times.

Achille Dévéria was a successful painter. The young people who went to the parties he gave adored dressing up. In 1830, Dévéria made a lithograph drawing of Alfred at twenty, dressed in the costume of a sixteenth-century page, looking as Romeo might have looked just before meeting Juliet.

Among the young men of fashion with whom he now spent so much of his time he found one or two who became more than mere companions in dissipation. Alfred Tattet, who was exactly his own age, was not merely a rich young man about town; he was also intelligent and capable of literary and artistic appreciation. He soon became one of the greatest admirers of Musset, the poet, and remained throughout his life his most intimate friend.

The number of Alfred's poems was steadily increasing and

he was beginning to think of publishing them. But first he published a very different kind of work. In his strange personality the frivolous and the macabre seemed always to dwell side by side. If his imagination was dazzled by the crystal chandeliers of elegant ballrooms, it was also nourished on strange dark fantasies completely alien to them. A Parisian publisher, a M. Mame, engaged him to make a French translation of an English 'novel'—of all books, *The Confessions of an Opium Eater*, by Thomas de Quincey. Alfred accepted the commission with alacrity and completed it in a month. But he did not trouble himself with the niceties of translation. For de Quincey's visions he substituted some of the horrible hallucinations he himself had experienced after beholding the corpses in the hospital mortuary. The book, published anonymously, aroused no interest at all. It appeared, then disappeared, Paul wrote, 'like a raindrop in the ocean'. But the phantoms that haunted Alfred's mind were not so easily dissipated.

Now, however, a very real and inescapable shock awaited him. Reality caught up with him in the person of his father who, less indulgent than his mother and elder brother, had for some time felt that Alfred's way of life was, to put it without exaggeration, unsatisfactory. M. de Musset, himself a civil servant keeping regular hours at his desk in the Ministry of War, was not prepared to allow his younger son to fritter away his time as a budding poet and dandy. He informed him one morning that he had found a post for him in the office of a M. Febvrel, the contractor for the central heating of military establishments. Alfred was obliged to obey his father's wishes and to betake himself dutifully to his office. His reaction to this distasteful situation, however, was both original and prompt. He gathered together his collection of verses, the manuscript of the *Contes d'Espagne et d'Italie*, on which he had been working quite seriously in spite of his apparent idleness, and took it to a publisher. The latter received it favourably but told him that he would need another five hundred lines to bring the manuscript up to the necessary length for publication.

'Five hundred lines!' Alfred exclaimed. 'If that's all I need to regain my freedom, you shall soon have them.'

It was summertime and Alfred's employer granted him three weeks' holiday. He went off on 27 August 1829, to

stay with his uncle Desherbiers at Le Mans. On 19 September
he returned to Paris and on that very evening read to Paul
his poem, *Mardoche*, which contained nearly six hundred
lines, and which he had written in those few weeks. M. Urbain
Canel, the publisher, was delighted and the manuscript was
immediately sent to the printer. The final proofs arrived
towards the end of the year. Alfred obtained his father's permission to invite some of his literary friends to a party on 24
December, when he read them three of the poems, all of which
were enthusiastically received by his guests, who included
several distinguished writers and poets, Prosper Mérimée
and Alfred de Vigny among them.

The volume was published almost immediately afterwards
and created a literary sensation. Not all the critics by any means
agreed with Sainte-Beuve's estimation of the poet's talent.
The Byronic influence on it was inescapably obvious. As
for the delightful *Ballade à la Lune*, certain pedantic old
gentlemen insisted on taking it seriously and with considerable
distaste. Alfred, however, had not written for their pleasure or
displeasure. The public whose approbation he sought consisted
of his contemporaries, the more intelligent and cultured young
men and women of his own generation and they did not fail
him. Now that he was a published poet invitations showered on
him; his social charm was enhanced by his romantic vocation.
Women sent him love-letters and invitations to rendezvous.
Among these was the following ingenuous note:

> Monsieur,
> A young Englishwoman who wishes to read your poems,
> is writing to you personally to ask you to let her have
> them. If you would be kind enough to send them to her,
> she would be greatly obliged.

This note seemed to Alfred to hint at more than it contained.
He promptly replied:

> Mademoiselle,
> As all young Englishwomen are pretty, I will not insult
> you by believing that you could be an exception to the rule,
> and, as you have so trustingly sent me your name and

address, do not be surprised if I give myself the honour of offering you in person the volume of poems you wish to read.

The situation was not, however, as romantic as Alfred assumed it to be. The young lady was the companion of the Duchesse de Castries, a high-born Frenchwoman who had asked the girl to get the book for her. Not knowing where else to apply for it, the ingenuous companion had written directly to the author. On receiving Alfred's gaily impudent acceptance of what he had assumed to be an invitation to another flirtation, the young lady confessed her error to the Duchesse who, greatly amused by this misunderstanding, ordered that when in due course the poet called he should be ushered into her salon. The Duchesse was by no means disagreeably impressed by the handsome young man, who, as she explained matters to him, soon overcame his embarrassment. Madame de Castries was one of the most charming and sought-after members of the aristocracy, and Alfred accepted her explanations with the best of grace. As a result of this unconventional meeting they became friends for life.

The most important result of the success of his poems, however, was his father's agreement that he might now be released from his clerical bondage and devote himself to a literary career. Nor was devotion an exaggerated term to use to describe the efforts he made to perfect his poetic style. Although he was not yet twenty, an age at which his pleasure in social life and his dandyism could be regarded with some indulgence, he was nevertheless completely in earnest in his determination to become a great poet and dramatist. He could take criticism, learn from his detractors, and now set out very seriously to improve his technical form, so much so that at twenty-four, less than five years later, he was generally acknowledged to be the most talented lyric poet of his generation.

The theatre had always attracted him. He had been waiting for the chance to make a career as a dramatist and when it came in the autumn of 1830 he seized on it eagerly. The director of the Odéon asked him for a play. He was delighted with the piece Musset wrote, which was entitled *La Nuit Vénitienne*. It was widely advertised, and the first production took place on 1 December. On this occasion, however, Alfred's luck, which had so highly favoured his poetic beginnings, completely deserted him. The first performance was wrecked by an irresistibly ludicrous incident.

The actress playing the romantic lead, wearing an immaculately white satin dress, had the misfortune to lean against one of the 'props', a trellis painted bright green—and not yet dry. When she turned her back to the audience they saw to their huge and harsh delight that her dress was covered from waist to ankles with large bright green squares. In the gusts of ribald laughter that ensued the actors were inaudible for the remainder of the performance. Although the trellis was promptly removed the play fared no better on its second night. It was a resounding flop. It was hardly surprising that Alfred, faced in his early youth with so bitter and ridiculous a failure, withdrew from the theatre in a rage of frustration. He continued nevertheless to write plays. But they appeared from then on only in print and none of them was performed, until, seventeen years later, by an equally fortuitous stroke of luck—but this time a happy one—the sensational success at the Comédie-Française of *Un Caprice* at last won him his rightful place as France's wittiest playwright since Marivaux.

6

In spite of the fact that Alfred in so many ways still remained the spoiled child who apparently refused to grow up, he was growing in mental maturity. Although his behaviour was often frivolous to the point of recklessness, and his imagination was even more inflammable than Byron's, he always retained the capacity for rational reflection and self-criticism. One evening in the autumn of 1830, when Paul had found him in deep meditation and asked him the reason for it, Alfred replied:

I am thinking that I have nearly reached my majority. Exactly two months from to-day I shall be twenty-one, and that's quite old. Do I really have to go about with so many young men, and listen to the gossipings of so many women, in order to understand them? Haven't I seen enough to be able to say plenty, if, that is, I have anything to say? Either there is nothing in one, in which case experience will not awaken anything in the mind, or else one has everything, in which case one need only know a little to be able to guess the rest. And yet I know that there is something more I need, although I do not know what it is. Perhaps a great love affair? Or a great misfortune? Possibly both of them. And for that I dare not hope. Experience is all very well—provided it does not kill one.

If Paul reported Alfred accurately on this occasion those words were certainly remarkable, for they were uncannily prophetic. Whether with some kind of extra-sensory premonition he knew it intuitively or not, Alfred was almost on the threshold of the great love affair that was to become the most famous episode of the Romantic period. Meanwhile, misfortune came first.

During the winter and early spring of 1832 Paris was stricken by a frightful epidemic of cholera.

It changed the entire appearance of the town [Paul wrote]. One could no longer go out without meeting hundreds of hearses. All night long there were everywhere signs of the pestilence—deserted streets lit from time to time by the red lanterns of the ambulances, shuttered shops, silence, a few horrified passers-by rushing out for help, and every morning the number of deaths had risen. By the spring of 1832 they amounted to a daily toll of fifteen hundred victims. Enormous removal vans at every door took away one or more coffins, some of them only half nailed down. If the bodies were not ready the overworked drivers protested at being kept waiting and argued with the relatives and servants. Paris had not witnessed such scenes since the Black Death in the reign of Charles V.

M. Victor de Musset, their father, was one of the victims of this terrible scourge. He was a literary man of distinction, an admirable and punctilious civil servant, well respected by his colleagues. In 1830, he had been dismissed from his post as

head of the Office of Military Justice. His colleagues addressed
a petition to the Minister for his reinstatement, emphasizing
his loyal service and the fact that he was the father of a family,
with no private means and no right to a pension. The petition
was successful and M. de Musset was retained in his post
with an annual salary of 8,000 francs. On 7 April 1832, he
had gone to his office as usual. His first symptoms occurred
when he returned home in the evening and by six o'clock the
next morning he was dead. His wife and children were stunned
by the shock, for they were an unusually devoted family and he
had been a model husband and an understanding father to his
growing sons. Even Alfred, to whom tears came easily, could
not weep. 'It was,' he said, 'one of those sorrows that tears
cannot soften, and the memory of which would always return
in all its bitterness and horror, for death strikes at our hearts
very differently from love.'

The loss of his father was also in the wider sense a disaster
for Alfred. In spite of his emotional temperament, his vaunted
passion for liberty, his hatred of an office stool and his determination to work only at literary creation, he was a dutiful
son. His father had been both kind and firm and such paternal
guidance was absolutely essential to act as a check on Alfred's
tendency to reckless extravagance, both emotional and
financial. Although Paul was five years older than Alfred and
filled with the best intentions to prove a worthy head of the
bereaved family, he was never able to exercise the restraining
influence of which his younger brother was so much in need.
Their father, veteran of the Napoleonic campaigns, also com-
manded his respect as a formerly glamorous warrior. Where
Alfred could have accepted certain disciplinary orders from
him, he never accepted anything from Paul beyond the
sympathy and the pecuniary help which he needed throughout
his life.

Paul, a staid young lawyer, was as much convinced of
Alfred's genius as their mother, possibly even more so. He was
his confidant, but never shared either in his social triumphs
or in his excursions into the underworld. Throughout Alfred's
life and after his death Paul remained his champion and
partisan. Undoubtedly there were occasions when his brilliant
younger brother's excesses shocked Paul, when he tried to

remonstrate, preach, or perhaps even scold a little. But Alfred's vices—for unfortunately they cannot be described more leniently—might not have taken so firm a hold on him had Paul not secretly derived a vicarious enjoyment from them. Paul spurred on what at first was probably no more than adolescent exhibitionism until excess in everything became Alfred's second nature. No doubt Paul's reactions to the situation were largely subconscious. Alfred's faults were excused on the grounds of his genius, his hyper-sensitivity and instability. Whenever, as he frequently did, he provoked opposition or antagonism, he invariably saw himself as the victim of some conspiracy. Occasionally there was truth in this view of the matter. But Paul too often sided with his brother and in doing so became unable to control him or help him to control himself.

At first the brothers thought that their father's death would mean a considerable straitening in the family's finances. Alfred met this situation with a characteristic mixture of common sense and romanticism:

> 'Unless one is well off,' [he told Paul one evening,] 'one can have no leisure, and without leisure there can be no poetry. . . . So this is what I have decided to do. I shall attempt one more volume of verse, which will have to be better than my first. If its publication does not bring me in, as I hope, enough to live on, I shall enlist in the Hussars of Chartres, or else in the Lancers. . . . I shall look well in uniform. I'm young and healthy. I like riding, and with the help of my friends it would be the very devil if I did not become an officer.'

He set to work in all seriousness and when at the end of a day he was pleased with what he had written he would say gleefully: 'I'm not a soldier yet.'

He produced two plays in verse, *La Coupe et les Lèvres* and *A quoi rêvent les jeunes filles*. The former bore the sub-title: '*Entre la coupe et les lèvres il reste encore de la place pour un malheur. (Proverbe ancien.)*' ('There's many a slip betwixt cup and lip.')

Several of Alfred's plays, both in prose and verse, were given such proverbial titles. The so-called *Proverbe* was a form that developed in French dramatic literature from eighteenth-century origins. It derived from the charades that were frequently acted in private, in country homes or drawing-rooms by amateurs, to their friends, who had to guess at the end of the performance which proverb the little piece represented. Alfred's *Proverbes*, also, developed from such amateur performances, in which he and his friends delighted.

But after the failure of *La Nuit Vénitienne* he continued to write his plays and *Proverbes* for arm-chair reading and not for performance. This second volume was also too short, by nearly one hundred pages. So he completed it by adding a long Byronic narrative poem, *Namouna*. The three works were published in one volume entitled *Spectâcle dans un fauteuil*, with a light-hearted dedication to the reader:

> Imagine, dear reader, your bad fairy's spite
> Made you purchase an Opera seat for to-night,
> You now have a gallery place or a stall,
> But what you will hear you do not know, at all.
>
> You may be amused, or equally, frown.
> The performers may weep or may laugh, whilst you yawn.
> Do not mind, it's the fashion, everyone goes,
> And somehow the time will pass, as it does.
>
> This book, my dear reader will, too, fill your leisure,
> Will cost just about the price of a stall,
> So open it kindly and read it with pleasure.
>
> If you like it or not, I pray you, be fair,
> A boring performance is common as air
> And mine you can watch without leaving your chair.

On publication the reviews were, with one exception, unenthusiastic. But that exception made all the difference. Sainte-Beuve once again came out with a long article in praise of the poet's talent. This appeared in the *Revue des deux Mondes* and turned the tide in Musset's favour. In spite of the flattering uniform of the Hussars of Chartres, he now no longer talked of enlisting. He was enrolled instead, among the contributors to that important literary review. The editor, Frédéric Buloz, continued with unswerving admiration and loyalty to publish all his writings—articles, criticisms, essays, poems, and plays until Alfred's death, frequently making him advances for them.

Now that Alfred was a professional man of letters, his hours of inspiration were regarded by his family as sacrosanct. The financial emoluments were very small and would not have sufficed to keep him. But it turned out that the family had been left better off than they had feared at the time of M. de Musset's death. They—Madame de Musset, Paul, Alfred, and their young sister Hermine—continued to live in the apartment in the Rue de Grenelle. His mother's pride and indulgence encircled Alfred like garlands of flowers. His tendencies to gamble and drink too much and to consort with women of easy virtue were for a long time hidden from her possibly averted gaze.

At twenty-three, Alfred de Musset's future beckoned brilliantly. Yet as he himself had felt two years previously, something was still lacking to bring his poetic talent to full fruition. 'Perhaps,' he had suggested to Paul, 'a great love affair?' Even had he foreseen that such an experience might wreck his whole life, it is unlikely that he would or could have evaded it. If, in order to become one of the world's greatest poets he would have to love and suffer as Dante, Abélard, and Byron had loved and suffered, he would still have chosen to become love's martyr for the sake of poetry.

⋙ III ⋘

Dawn of Love

I

IN THE spring of 1833 Buloz, editor of the *Revue des deux
Mondes*, decided to invite all his contributors to a dinner
party to celebrate its second anniversary. Distinguished as
many of them were, they must on the whole have been socially
a somewhat dingy lot. But there were also at this party—which
only for this reason became a landmark in French literary
history—two contributors of a very different kind. One of them
was Alfred de Musset; the other, Madame George Sand, the
only woman present. It was their first meeting.

Alfred de Musset, now an established poet, was nevertheless
still the gay, reckless, high-spirited young dandy. He had
grown extraordinarily handsome, with a mass of burnished
gold hair, flashing eyes, an irresistible smile and an inexhaustible fund of gaiety and malice. He was still dressed by the
most expensive tailors in Paris in the latest masculine fashion:
in a frock coat with an enormous velvet collar, tight, sky-blue
trousers, and tall hat, set rakishly to one side. His youthful
panache reflected both the springtime of his life and the
dangerous charm of Paris in that loveliest of seasons.

Alfred was not, however, a true dandy, according to a
connoisseur of the lighter side of Parisian life under Louis-
Philippe, Henri d'Alméras, who, in *La Vie Parisienne sous le
Règne de Louis-Philippe*, wrote:

> Women are much more susceptible to masculine beauty
> than they would like us to think, or will admit. The least
> details do not escape them. If one asked a woman in love
> able to speak the truth about this, she would reply that it
> was neither the cut of his coat nor the colour of his

44

waist-coat that attracted her to her loved one. They no
doubt pay attention to clothes, but if their choice lay
between a handsome and badly dressed young man
and an ugly one, however well turned out, the suggestion
that they might prefer the latter would be a mere tailors'
story.

de Musset . . . was a man lucky in love and not always
worthy of this most enviable privilege, but he was not, in
the fullest sense of the word, a dandy. His manners and
appearance were distinguished, he had a head of beautiful
fair hair; his expression when he was amongst men was
often bored and sullen, yet, on the contrary, with women
he was charming, brimming over with youthfulness, delicious verve and invention, very light-hearted and very
gamin. He obviously preferred their society to that of
men, even the most intelligent men, and he was perfectly
right.

He was also too impressionable, too emotional, too
excessive, and in a word, too French, to be a real dandy.
He did not and could not have that impassivity, that
impeccable correctitude of a London gentleman, imitated
more or less badly by the 'lions' of Paris. He also lacked,
and this was more serious, the art of dressing well.

To which M. d'Alméras added this charming footnote:

It was no doubt this serious gap in his education
that prevented him from being admitted to the Jockey
Club.

Alfred had given his whimsical gaiety full rein in *Fantasio*,
the prose play that followed *Les Caprices de Marianne*. It is
set in an imaginary Munich in the Middle Ages, when the
King of Bavaria's lovely daughter Elsbeth is about to wed
the Prince of Mantua in order to avoid a war between her
own and his states. Fantasio, a young citizen seeking refuge
from his creditors, disguises himself by means of an artificial
hump and a wig and succeeds the old Court Jester who
has died. The Prince, wanting unofficially to meet his fiancée,
changes places with one of his courtiers. Elsbeth is distressed

at the thought of having to marry that repugnant elderly man; Fantasio, to save her, whisks away the alleged Prince's wig with a fishing-rod. The real Prince departs in dudgeon. The only 'moral' appears to be that a broken peace is better than a lovely maiden's broken heart. But the charm of the play lies in the character and the lines spoken by Fantasio, who is the very incarnation of gay, reckless youth; a self-portrait of his author at the age of twenty-three, all romance and high spirits.

Alfred, not surprisingly, was far from being generally popular or admired by his colleagues. He refused to fit into any literary coterie or category. After he had withdrawn from the *Cénacle* he had gone his own individual way as a writer, and spent most of his leisure time in either the highest or lowest society. In spite of his undeniable poetic talents, which all his rivals had had to concede, he was not a serious young man of letters, not *sérieux*. Their disapprobation was barely concealed. They were aware of his debaucheries, of his excursions into the underworld of brothels and prostitutes, of his addiction to alcohol. Alfred was still young enough to enjoy a reputation for evil-living almost as much as his wickedness itself, though it is in fact doubtful if he ever did enjoy the latter. In the Romantic Age it was almost obligatory for any Byronic young dandy's self-respect that he should earn himself the name of libertine. Sainte-Beuve, who, although he was Madame Hugo's acknowledged lover, was himself demure and prudish to the point of priggishness, was, like Paul, fascinated by Alfred's glamour and impressed by his talent. But most of his colleagues took a less favourable view.

A few years previously, when in Dévéria's salon Alfred had danced with his two charming young partners, he had met there a man of letters, Gustave Planche, who was now the leading critic on the *Revue des deux Mondes*. Almost at first sight the two men had taken an irrevocable dislike to one another. Planche, who was unattractive and grubby to the point of uncleanliness, had not danced, but sat in a corner scowling at the handsome young partner of the prettiest girls present, and spreading malicious gossip about him. At that time Alfred had merely despised Planche, who had become the devoted slave of Madame Sand, with whom, it was generally

Alfred de Musset, medallion by David d'Angers (1830)

Portrait of Byron by Alfred de Musset as an art student

assumed, he was living. Their antipathy was shortly to turn
into real enmity.

Alfred found most of the others nearly as boring, pompous,
badly dressed and vulgarian. He made fun of them in witty
lines and caricatures, both verbally and in drawings that had
more than a slight touch of cruelty in their dissecting observation. Although he had thrown away his medical student's
scalpel in horror, his pencil could be almost as sharp. And it
was not used on corpses but on living subjects whom it could
hurt.

Alfred at this time never thought of a woman as a person,
a human being, but merely as a female who fitted into one or
another social and sexual category. He venerated his mother;
he admired several aristocratic ladies, such as the Duchesse de
Castries. He was always, even when very young, touched by
the innocent charm of pretty, well-bred girls. Never in his life
until now had he met a *femme de lettres*, a woman writer. It
was a new experience, and new experiences were the life's
blood of his youthful inspiration.

Yet when Buloz deliberately—and according to all accounts
maliciously—at this dinner placed M. de Musset next to
Madame Sand, Alfred saw in his neighbour, at first, at any
rate, only another woman. It was quite usual for young men of
the day to sum up a woman's 'points' like those of a filly.
So as he glanced with well-bred, controlled curiosity at his
neighbour, it was her appearance rather than her literary
reputation that interested him.

He saw a quiet young woman, aged twenty-nine,
simply and neatly dressed, with a mass of black hair
and enormous, dark, pansy-velvet eyes. She spoke very little
but appeared to listen intelligently. George Sand had no
conversational gifts; her talent expressed itself exclusively in
writing.

Alfred, who needed the presence of a woman in order to
appear at his best, displayed his gifts—his wit, charm, high
spirits—as a peacock might display before a demure, quiet
little peahen. But in fact George was as demure as the Mona
Lisa, and Alfred, as he set himself out to please her, from
vanity as much as for any other reason, could never, in the
youthful *naïveté* which still underlay his outward sophistication,

D

have guessed what was passing in the mind of that subtle and
enigmatic creature.

2

George Sand is to-day no longer very much read, except by
French students obliged to include some of her novels in their
curriculum and by literary experts. Yet if her works, like those
of George Eliot, who was born fifteen years later and became in
some ways her English counterpart, tend to remain honour-
ably on library shelves, her personality has never ceased to
fascinate millions who have never read a line she wrote, as much
as it fascinated her contemporaries on whom her earlier novels
especially made an indelible impression.

Her real name was Aurore Dupin. Her ancestry embodied
a whole series of seventeenth- and eighteenth-century romances,
of alliances between aristocrats and proletarians, legitimate and
illegitimate.

She had inherited the enormous dark eyes as well as the
name of her great-great-grandmother, Aurore de Koenigs-
marck, mistress of the Elector of Saxony, Frederick-Augustus,
to whom she bore a son in 1696—Maurice, Maréchal de
Saxe, one of the more romantic eighteenth-century soldiers,
as famous for his amours as for his military prowess. This general
kept a company of young actresses on the pay-roll, who even
on the eve of battle gave nightly theatrical performances. In
1748, one of Maurice de Saxe's mistresses bore him a daughter,
Marie-Aurore, who was legally married, twice; first to an
officer named Augustus de Horne and secondly in 1778, to a
M. Dupin de Francueil, aged sixty-two, who had previously
for years been her aunt's lover. Although Marie-Aurore was
thirty years younger than her second husband the marriage
was a great success. A son, another Maurice, was born. M.
Dupin died before the Revolution, leaving his widow with a
substantial income. Paris in 1793 was no place for a lady who
had been a *protégée* of the Dauphine, and who was mixed up
in allegedly counter-revolutionary activities. After only
narrowly escaping the Terror, Madame Dupin bought a
country estate in Berry called Nohant, and retired there with
her son and his tutor, the Abbé Deschartres.

Maurice, also a soldier, never achieved the distinction of his famous grandfather. His morals, however, were no less broad-minded. In 1800, when he was serving as a young aide-de-camp in Milan, he met the mistress of his general, a very pretty creature, Antoinette-Sophie-Victoire Delaborde. She promptly deserted the general for his young and attractive aide. Sophie was a truly proletarian camp-follower, whose father had once kept an estaminet and later sold canaries and finches on the Paris quays. Madame Dupin was horrified to learn from her only and adored son that they were married. They were then living in Paris. Sophie was about to give birth to a child, whom Maurice wished to legitimize. On the evening of 1 July 1804, he was playing the violin, whilst his happy young wife danced a quadrille. In the midst of the dance her pains took her. She retired to the next room and almost immediately a daughter was born, a third Aurore, who was in due course to become famous under a masculine pseudonym—George Sand.

Little Aurore Dupin was lucky to have been born in wedlock. Each of her parents already had an illegitimate child—her father, a son, Hippolyte Châtiron, by one of the maids at Nohant; her mother, a daughter by a former lover. With such an ancestry George Sand's multiple amorous adventures were almost inevitable, especially as Aurore Dupin grew up as attractive and sexually voracious as both her parents.

Her grandmother was deeply distressed by Maurice's *mésalliance* and took an ineluctible dislike to her common daughter-in-law, which was entirely reciprocated. Maurice had hoped to win his mother over by bringing his wife and children to Nohant after the Spanish campaign. For Sophie had at that time given birth to a son, who, had he not died in infancy, would have become the heir. This, also, was a stroke of good fortune for his elder little sister, Aurore. Soon after their arrival at Nohant, Maurice Dupin was killed in a riding accident.

Madame Dupin now had no heir, only an heiress. She accepted the situation and the child. But her vulgarian mother and her illegitimate daughter she could not accept. Sophie was sent back to Paris. Aurore remained at Nohant, which, on her grandmother's death and the attainment of her majority, became her property.

When Aurore was fourteen Madame Dupin placed her in
the convent of the Dames Augustines Anglaises in Paris, which
had been founded by English nuns who had fled to Catholic
France from Puritan England. Aurore, unused to discipline
and rebellious by nature, at first became one of the little
'devils'—the naughty smallest girls who promptly made her
their ringleader. But a year later, when puberty came, she
suffered the metamorphoses usual to intelligent emotional
girls of fifteen—her mind was submerged in religious ecstasy
and her heart was given to Mother Mary-Alicia, the most
beautiful of the nuns. She imagined ever afterwards that she
had experienced a genuine religious conversion. Her temperament, however, was totally unfitted to such a vocation, as her
spiritual directors well knew.

She was her grandmother's heiress and in 1821 the old
lady, anxious to get Aurore married before her own approaching death, took her back to Nohant. Her father's old tutor,
the Abbé Deschartres, had always felt that Aurore should
have been a boy, and it was a boy's training he now gave her.
He took her out riding and shooting and for these expeditions
he very easily persuaded the girl to wear a man's clothes. For
the rest of her life she did so whenever the mood took her.
As she grew up the masculine side of her nature came more
and more into the ascendant. She was inexhaustibly strong
and wiry. In spite of her feminine charms—those enormous
sentimental eyes, thick black hair, a golden peach-like skin
and a neat little figure, her character became increasingly
self-willed and domineering. She had no nerves at all and was
mentally and physically fearless. Old Deschartres, who had
become Mayor of Nohant and also doctored all the local
inhabitants, made Aurore his assistant. There was apparently
no incongruity between her masculinity of character and dress
and her passion for nursing. Like any male medical student—
excepting that over-sensitive young poet, Alfred de Musset—
she took it all in her stride: accidents, ailments, fevers and their
physical symptoms, such as bleeding and suffering.

It was then, during her seventeenth year, that her character
was formed into a mould which never changed.

Her grandmother died in 1821. It was necessary to find her
a husband as quickly as possible. In September 1822 she married

Casimir Dudevant, a rather stupid young man, the illegitimate but acknowledged son of the Baron Dudevant, and went home to Nohant with him. But although she was the owner of the property, on her marriage her legal rights in it passed to her husband. In June 1823, a son, a third Maurice, was born in Paris, where they had gone for her confinement.

Aurore was much more intelligent than her husband and never let him forget it. She was also now a married woman, extremely attractive to and constantly attracted by other men. She first had a platonic friendship—with her husband's reluctant consent—with a young Bordeaux lawyer, Aurélien de Sèze, and soon afterwards a genuine love affair with a young neighbour, Stéphane de Grandsagne, who, rumour claimed, was the father of her second child, a daughter, Solange, born in 1828 at Nohant. By this time Casimir had taken to drink, like Aurore's half-brother, Hippolyte Châtiron, his boon companion, and to sleeping with the chambermaids. A separation was agreed on. Aurore was yearning to escape from the deadly boredom of Nohant to the stimulating atmosphere of Paris. In 1830, she had met at the neighbouring small town of La Châtre a young law student, Jules Sandeau. She was now twenty-six, he, a handsome curly-haired little fellow of nineteen. She became his mistress and joined him in Paris, where from 1831 onwards she made her home.

She was obliged to exist on a very small allowance from her husband, which she decided to supplement by writing novels in collaboration with young Sandeau. Aurore had always been a voluminous scribbler and now she set herself to learn the trade of writing in earnest. Together they produced one or two novels under the joint pseudonym of J. Sand. But her talent, the richness and vivacity of her imagination far outstripped that of the poor lad who had willy-nilly become her collaborator both in love and in literature. Her first independent novel, *Indiana*, was published in 1832. As her own pseudonym she chose, not the French Georges but the English George Sand, and retained it for the rest of her life. She had reached maturity. Her dawn was over and never again did she refer to herself as Aurore.

3

Indiana was an instant success, largely owing to an
enthusiastic review in the newly founded *Revue des deux Mondes*
by its foremost literary critic, Gustave Planche. His enthusiasm
for its author was no less steadfast. He adored her and soon
became her devoted slave. It was Planche who introduced Sand
to the review's editor, Frédéric Buloz.

Now, at last she achieved her independence. Buloz engaged
her as a regular contributor to the *Revue des deux Mondes*; her
publishers, delighted with the success of *Indiana*, paid her
fifteen hundred francs advance for her next novel, *Valentine*.
Another of her admirers, Henri de Latouche, lent her his
apartment on the Quai Malaquais.

George Sand, now a famous novelist and journalist, was
soon the latest fashion amongst French men of letters, for in
her time a professional woman writer was still something of a
literary rarity. Balzac, de Vigny, and others paid her attention,
the latter unfavourably. George had struck up one of her
passionate-sentimental friendships with women, with Marie
Dorval, the poet's mistress, a lovely and talented actress.
In his *Journal d'un Poète*, de Vigny gave the following description of George at that time:

> She would seem to be about twenty-five. Her appearance
> is that of the famous *Judith* in the Gallery. Her black and
> curling hair falls over her collar in the manner of one
> of Raphael's angels. Her eyes are large and dark, their
> shape such as is to be found in mystics and in the most
> magnificent Italian faces. Her features are severe and
> impassive. The chin is less pleasing, the mouth badly
> formed. There is an absence of elegance in her bearing
> and her speech is harsh. She looks and talks like a man,
> and has the voice and forthrightness of one. . . .

It was obvious that by this time George Sand had
outstripped, both intellectually and emotionally, Aurore's
effeminate youthful lover, Sandeau. Her work now became her
refuge from and substitute for more intimate emotions. She

formed the habit of writing a steady number of thousands of words every night, from which she never afterwards deviated, whether in sickness or in health, in or out of love. Sandeau, poor lad, still adored her. First, she sent him to live by himself in the Rue de l'Université. But this was not far away enough. So long as Jules remained in Paris she would continue to feel remorseful about him. He must, she decided, go farther away, away from France altogether, to Italy. The discarded collaborator struggled as helplessly as a dying butterfly in the net of a collector. He attempted to commit suicide by swallowing acetate of morphine but it only made him sick. Herself sickened by his futile struggles, his captor took the necessary steps to eliminate him. She made all arrangements for his departure; packed for him, got him a passport and a seat in the coach, and even lent him the money to pay his fare.

Aurore Dupin-George Sand was as much a dual personality as Alfred de Musset. She, too, contained in herself a romantic tender-hearted Coelio and a merciless, realistic, ruthless Octave, who allowed nothing to impede his aims. In order to salve Aurore-Coelio's conscience, Octave-George told herself that the end of her affair with Sandeau was due to his unfaithfulness. Having invented this story she stuck to it and believed in it as firmly as her admirers believed in her printed autobiographical fiction. Even the staunchest of them were at first slightly appalled by the summary end of her romance with Sandeau.

Tant pis!

Among these literary friends the most important and potentially useful was Sainte-Beuve. George soon chose him as a 'confessor', a role he was delighted to fill. He was an acute observer and critic of human foibles and this extraordinary young woman, who had already made such a striking success of her career and at the same time an equally great failure of her love life, was a unique specimen for study.

For George could not live without love. She was both a romantic of her generation, a romantic by temperament and —for her time—a pioneer. It is easy for twentieth-century students of that period to analyse the character of a so-called feminist. In George Sand's day the science of psychology had not yet been born. Yet with that mental as well as physical fearlessness which was her most admirable characteristic she was capable, within the limits of then existing knowledge, of analysing her experiences, her longings and needs, and of setting down the conclusions she came to in novel form, however shocking they might appear to her contemporaries. It was beyond her knowledge to discover such concepts as 'inferiority complex', or the 'sub-conscious', 'repressions', 'ego', 'id', or to interpret the aspects of human nature to which Freud so very much later gave these definitions. What she knew and fearlessly stated in print was that a woman, like a man, had physical needs which had to find fulfilment in sexual intercourse. If love meant anything at all, then the divine element in it, the spiritual union of twin-souls, must find its counterpart in a mutually satisfactory physical union. She now proceeded to embody this theory in a novel, *Lélia*. George already knew from experience that in her own personality there was a hard core that none of her lovers, until then, had ever been able to master. It was always she who dominated them. Yet she remained a Katharine, still hopefully longing for and seeking her Petruchio. The one she now chose was Prosper Mérimée. He saw himself rather as a Don Juan, a man of sexual experience and sensual prowess which most women found irresistible. The fact that George had never yet known sensual pleasure was a challenge which he set himself to meet. She, with her extraordinary mixture of romanticism and matter-of-factness, was at that time so utterly defeated in her search for love that she agreed to Mérimée's suggestion which, bluntly, amounted to a proposal that she should seek it by way of lust.

But George had no feminine wiles, no techniques with which to match those of this odd, cynical voluptuary. When they made the attempt it was a wretched, ridiculous failure. Mérimée claimed that by her lack of such seductive routine she had so completely stripped him of all desire that he became impotent. George, with that realism which never, even in her moments of defeat and mortification, deserted her wrote to Sainte-Beuve that

I behaved, at thirty, as no girl of fifteen would ever have done. . . . The experiment failed completely. I wept

> from sheer nervous exhaustion, disgust and despondency . . .
> I found myself confronted by bitter, superficial mockery. . . .

The mockery went all round literary Paris. But George, who in spite of the appalling frustration she had suffered could still coldly write about this affair as an experiment, would nevertheless not give up her quest. Sex without love was hell; love without sex would have been heaven. But with both her feet so firmly planted on earth, however much her head may have been in the sky, she felt that there must be a solution for her longings somewhere, if only she could find it. She dreamed of a man who would give her both romantic and physical satisfaction, who would inflame her heart, satisfy the aspirations of her soul, and awaken her senses. Somewhere, surely, he must exist.

Sainte-Beuve attempted to help her in this quest. He was sincerely attached to her; admired her intellect, integrity and uncommon industry. Yet in spite of these, in spite of her predilection for wearing men's clothes, of her originality and daring, she seemed to him ineluctably feminine. As a gallant Frenchman he could not leave this poor little woman, so hungry to love and be loved, unconsoled, although he himself was in no position to console her. His chivalry was not without a tinge of alarmed self-interest. For George, with her usual directness, had made it clear that she would have been prepared to accept him as a possible candidate for her affections. His, however, were already placed elsewhere. During that summer of 1833 she was constantly writing him letters, notes, to which he prudently refrained from replying; and for a whole month he had not been to see her:

> There may be two alternative reasons [she wrote to him in July 1833] for this: one of them is probable and depressing, the other silly and ridiculous. The first is that I bore you, that you find in my desperate nature an embarrassing spectacle which sometimes disturbs your youthful confidence in life and therefore you avoid my disagreeable company: I can understand that.
> The second is, that you are in love with some jealous woman who does me the honour to consider me a rival

and has forbidden you to see me. That would be very funny. If it is true, can you not reassure her, tell her that I am three hundred years old, that I ceased to be a woman before her own grandmother was born . . . that I am no use at anything except psychological discussions which no more attract men to me than myself to them. . . .

This and other letters reveal a certain disingenuousness and clumsiness, in no way concealing the writer's eagerness to have her theories as to the possible reasons for her friend's caution proved wrong. Sainte-Beuve was far too canny either to be deceived or tempted by them. So that as much in self-protection as in pity he set about trying to canalize George's unused emotions in some other direction. He had always admired Alfred de Musset; to him he seemed an Adonis in appearance, a charmer of charmers. Would George not, he suggested to her, like to meet this enchanting young poet? No, she would not. For she was aware of his reputation as a dandy, a young lion of the salons, a social favourite. She herself was a deeply serious young woman, completely bohemian in dress and straightforward in manner:

> . . . By the way, having thought it over, I do not want you to bring Musset. He is very much the dandy, we would not have anything in common, and I was more curious than interested in meeting him. I think it may be imprudent to want to gratify one's curiosity on every occasion, and better to follow one's inclinations. . . .

She asked Sainte-Beuve to bring instead, Dumas, who had wished to call on her. They became friends, but no more; Dumas, an inveterate gossip, made merciless fun of her fiasco with Mérimée, and later said that in *Lélia* George Sand had dished out Byronism 'by the kilo'.

George afterwards declared that, knowing Alfred de Musset was to be present at Buloz's dinner-party, she had nearly decided not to attend it. Neither of them ever claimed that they had met through some romantic freak of fate. But it is almost certain that her curiosity about Musset was greater than she had admitted in her letter to Sainte-Beuve.

Their fellow-guests undoubtedly found the situation piquant. Gustave Planche probably enjoyed the party least of all. For by that time he was almost permanently installed in George's apartment. In spite of her denials, all her colleagues assumed him to be her lover. In view of Planche's unprepossessing appearance and manners George was probably telling the truth. Nevertheless she made constant use of him as a general amanuensis and errand-boy; as escort, as 'baby-sitter' to her little daughter Solange, to take her son to school, and even to accompany her husband to the theatre on the rare occasions when he came to Paris from Nohant and she was too busy writing to go out with him.

The rest of the company would not have been Frenchmen and journalists, all working on the same review, zealously exchanging news and gossip, had this meeting between their one and only woman colleague and young Alfred de Musset not titivated their malice.

But instead of the affected and conceited dandy George had expected to meet, she found herself sitting next to *Fantasio* —a delightfully amusing youth, bubbling over with high spirits and almost childish gaiety. 'A mere child . . . ' that was her first and lasting impression of Alfred. As in the case of Jules Sandeau, she immediately felt herself his elder and better; his superior in intellect and experience. Although previously she had been in despair for want of love, almost as soon as she met Alfred she thought that she was only impelled to influence him for his own good. She had by now firm theories on almost every subject that interested and perplexed her contemporaries —on religion (she believed in God or Divine inspiration, but not in the restraints imposed by the Church)—on politics (she was a liberal veering to the idealistic socialism of her day) —on women and their responsibilities both to themselves and to society.

Alfred, needless to say, was neither attracted by George's views or theories, nor by her good intentions, with which their joint road to hell was from now on to be paved.

Although on this occasion George Sand was wearing feminine dress, she could not entirely deprive herself of at least one eccentricity: fastened to her belt she wore a little dagger, which Alfred found very amusing. He was more than amused,

however, by her physical attraction. Those huge dark eyes
that even de Vigny could not help admiring, that thick
lustrous black hair, her peach-like skin, almost Mediterranean
in tint, appealed instantly to his senses. For in his very earliest
poems he had already dreamed of such dark, luscious beauty,
of a 'swan-like neck' and 'a bosom, golden as the young
vine'.

He re-read George Sand's *Indiana*. He then sent her the
following note:

> Madame,
>   I take the liberty of sending you herewith a few verses
> that I wrote after re-reading a chapter of *Indiana*, the
> one in which Noun receives Raimond in her mistress's
> room. Their slight value would have made me hesitate
> to present them to your gaze, did they not offer me an
> opportunity to express the sincere and profound admiration
> which inspired them.

This letter, flattering yet extremely respectful, enclosed a
poem of eight and a half verses in a very different vein. For,
taking advantage of poetic licence, its author addressed the
author of *Indiana* in the second person singular. The
intimacy of this form of address is impossible to reproduce in
our language, as is the voluptuousness of the lines themselves.

George replied in equally admiring vein but refusing to
answer his questions more directly than in referring him to
Lélia, with an oblique reference to the 'sad secrets' of her
past. She ended:

> When I had the honour of meeting you I did not dare
> to invite you to visit me. I still fear that the severity of my
> home would repel and bore you. However, if in a moment
> of fatigue and distaste for social activity you would care to
> enter a recluse's cell, you would be received there with
> gratitude and cordiality.

George invariably made a point of stressing her sorrows
and the asceticism of her life and setting. And it was true that
she had in herself no reserves whatever of humour or self-

entertainment. For gaiety and amusement she relied solely on the high spirits and sense of fun of her friends and admirers. When Musset promptly took advantage of her carefully worded invitation, it was as if the tiny garret flat on the Quai Malaquais where she then lived was suddenly flooded with sunshine.

Yet both of them were still fencing, not only with one another but with the increasingly passionate emotions they were beginning to feel. Was this to be the great love affair for which Alfred had been yearning? After reading *Lélia* in proof, he wrote George a remarkable letter, admiring, devoted, and yet containing both a confession and an underlying warning:

> You know me well enough by now to be sure that the ridiculous words—will you or won't you?—will never pass my lips in your case. There is the whole Baltic sea between us in this respect—you can only love on a moral plane, whilst I could never love anyone like that (even supposing that were I to ask you to, you would not straightaway throw me out)—but I can be—should you consider me worthy of it—not even your friend, that would still be too moral for me—but a kind of comrade of no importance and with no rights, consequently without jealousy and without scenes, who would smoke your tobacco, rumple your gowns, and be prepared to catch cold whilst philosophizing with you under all the chestnut trees of modern Europe. If then, when you had nothing better to do, or felt like being foolish (how polite I am!) you would like my company for an hour or an evening . . . I would be dealing with my dear Monsieur George Sand, who from now onwards is for me a man of genius. Forgive me for saying so to your face, I have no reason to lie to you.
>
> With all my heart,
> Alfd de Musset.

It was the last fence between them. Within a matter of days Alfred himself kicked it away and gave his heart for better or worse into George's keeping.

They had been on another long walk together, when they

had been discussing George's future plans, which included a possible journey to Italy.

My dear George,
    I have something silly and ridiculous to tell you. I am stupidly writing to you, I don't know why, instead of having told it you when we came back from that walk. I shall be in despair tonight. You will laugh in my face and take me for a mere phrase-maker in all my dealings with you until now. You will show me the door and think that I am lying. I am in love with you. I have been, since the first day I went to see you. I thought that by seeing you solely as a friend I would cure myself of it. There are a lot of things in your character that could have cured me; I tried to persuade myself of it as best I could, but I am paying too dearly for the hours I spend with you. I prefer to tell you, and I am right, because now I shall suffer much less in curing myself after you have closed your door to me. Last night I had decided to let you know that I had gone away and was in the country, but I do not want to make any mysteries nor to appear to have quarrelled with you without any reason. Now you will say, George: here's another bore, as you do say! but if I mean anything at all to you, tell me what to do, as you would have told me yesterday, when we were talking of someone else. But if you doubt the truth of what I am telling you, then, please, do not reply at all. I know what you think of me and I hope for nothing in saying this. I cannot bear to lose a friend or to give up the only happy hours I have been spending for the past month. But I know that you are kind, that you have been in love, and I rely on you, not as a mistress, but as on a frank and loyal comrade. George, I am a madman to deprive myself of the pleasure of seeing you during the short time you will be remaining in Paris before you leave for the country and Italy, where we could have spent such lovely nights if only I had the strength. But the truth is that I am suffering and am not strong enough.

A second letter followed soon afterwards, when he had finished reading the proofs of *Lélia*. This letter was later badly mutilated, several passages having been cut out with scissors. Those that remain, however, appear to refer to a meeting at which George had reproached Alfred. In spite of the obvious sincerity of the previous two letters, the almost adolescent naïveté of the second, she was not yet, apparently, completely reassured as to his reliability. She was already in love with Coelio, but feared Octave:

You remember telling me one day that when someone had asked you if I was Octave or Coelio you had answered: both, I think.—My folly has been only to show you one of them, George. . . . Whose fault was it? Mine. Pity my sad disposition for having been used to living in a closed coffin, and hate those who forced me into it. This, you said yesterday, is a prison wall; everything would break against it. Yes, George, there is a wall; you only forgot one thing, that behind it is a prisoner.

That is my whole story, my past and future life. It will do me a lot of good, I shall be very happy, when I shall have scribbled bad rhymes all over the walls of my cell! It's a fine thing to remain dumb when one is with the being who could understand one, and to create a sacred treasure out of one's suffering, which one then throws out into the streets, into the drains, at six francs a time!

Be sorry for me, do not despise me. As I have not been able to explain myself to you, I shall die silent. If my name is written in a corner of your heart, however faintly, do not rub it out. I can embrace a foul and dead-drunk prostitute, but I cannot embrace my mother.

Love those who know how to love, I only know how to suffer. There are days when I could kill myself; but I weep, or else I burst out laughing, although certainly not today. Adieu, George, I love you like a child.

This letter, which contains the very essence of Coelio-Octave, also fixed once and for all the relationship between them. 'Mother'—'child'—those are the words of capital importance. Alfred had not, in spite of his sincere desire to do so, been seeking a comrade, a friend, a 'brother' in George Sand, but a mother-surrogate. In writing that he could not embrace his mother and that this drove him into the arms of prostitutes, he unconsciously revealed his repressed conflict, the guilt feelings which were the source of his inner tension and its outward manifestation, from time to time, in hysteria.

To George he was her 'child', her 'little boy', her *gamin*.

She was twenty-nine, six years older than he, married, a mother of two young children, the previous mistress of several lovers—the one woman with whom his sub-conscious passionately wanted a mock-incestuous relationship.

Whenever in future Coelio's guilt-feelings overcame him Octave would get drunk, make a violent scene, after which the tensions would be temporarily resolved as a tearful and repentant Coelio implored his 'mother' on his knees to forgive him—but to begin all over again.

Later he was to write:

O, Muse! Que m'importe ou la mort ou la vie!
J'aime, et je veux pâlir; j'aime et je veux souffrir . . .

But first he had to live his love and his suffering. At twenty-three he had found the great love affair he had anticipated at seventeen, which was to break his heart but to bring his genius to its full flowering.

Self-caricature illustrating '*Ballade à la Lune*'

Drawing of Alfred de Musset as a young dandy

⫸⫸⫸ IV ⫷⫷⫷

The spectre of Fontainebleau

A NEW lover and a new novel—George was in heaven and
felt ten years younger. For *Lélia* was published almost
as soon as she had become Alfred's mistress. Although he was
still officially living at home, he was spending nearly all his
time at George's apartment. This consisted of four tiny little
attics, all in a row, at the very top of the magnificent mansion
that had belonged to her great-grandfather, the famous
Maréchal de Saxe. Their ceilings were so low, no higher than
five-foot-five or six, that few of her male visitors could have
stood up straight in them without bumping their heads. Each
little attic had a dormer window that looked out on a magnificent view. To the right, only a few doors away on the quayside,
stood the Institut de France, and across the Pont des Arts, over
the river, was the Palace of the Tuileries with formal gardens,
in which George or Planche when she was too busy, writing,
could take her children to play. When they were not together
he wrote poems to her—even in his bath:

> Love, supremest delight I thought I had banned,
> Azure-eyed angel with downcast lids,
> Now returned at last in the star-studded night,
> With your tender smile, your eyes filled with tears,
> Once again at my bedside you stand.
> I had cursed you, and drove you away for three years,
> Well, two words that you spoke made me king of this world.
> Put your hand on the wound in my heart and its pain,
> Re-open it, so that it breaks in my breast.
> Never lover adored, bending over his love
> In two darker eyes drank celestial delight
> Nor a lovelier forehead his lips e'er caressed.

George's friends and hangers-on were, naturally, by no
means as enraptured as she was by this youthful intruder into

their circle. Her small home was generally full of them.
Boucoiran, Maurice's tutor, was there most of the time.
There was no dislodging Gustave Planche, who continued
to hover around like a nasty blue-bottle in Love's ointment.
Alfred, in the highest spirits, drew wicked caricatures of them,
lampooned them in verses which delighted George:

> George is in her attic,
> Smoking a cigarette,
> Between two pots of flowers,
> With tears her eyes are wet.
>
> Buloz, on the floor beside her,
> Kind words provides, and looks.
> Solange, just behind her,
> Is scribbling in her books.
>
> Boucoiran, a muddy milestone,
> Is staring with a frown
> At Musset, who, quite crazy,
> Fools, and plays the clown.
>
> Planche, sitting in the corner,
> Still drunk from yesterday,
> Is cleaning out his ear
> In the most meticulous way.

He also played absurd pranks and practical jokes, such as
dressing-up as a maidservant and at dinner pretending by
accident to pour a jug of cold water over one of her more
decorous guests, the philosopher Lerminier. A mere but
adorable *gamin*. . . .

Lélia created a sensation which, however, was not entirely
favourable. Among the critics whom its outspokenness, which
they thought amounted to licentiousness, deeply shocked, was
Capo de Feuillide, the reviewer of *La Vie Littéraire*, who,
among other aspersions on its authoress wrote that the lips
[sic] that had uttered such shameless and disgusting thoughts
should be sealed with red-hot coals! In the 1830's it was usual
for writers who felt themselves insulted by such unfavourable
reviews to challenge their critics to a duel. (The resultant

publicity was by no means damaging to their sales.) But in spite of her masculine pseudonym and dress, George Sand was unable to exchange her pen for a sword. The wretched Planche, hoping perhaps thereby to win back her favour, jumped in where his angel was unable to tread, and challenged Feuillide on her behalf. When Alfred heard this he was not surprisingly furious at Planche's attempt to usurp what he felt was now his right.

George herself, not displeased by the sensation *Lélia* was causing, nevertheless took a completely feminine and sensible view of this ridiculous affair. She wrote to Sainte-Beuve, asking him to reply in the only rational manner to Feuillide, in a favourable review in the *National*. At the same time she took the opportunity to write to him about a matter much closer to her heart:

25 August [1833]

I have fallen in love and this time very seriously, with Alfred de Musset. This is no longer a caprice; it is a serious attachment. . . . I was once in love for six years and another time for three, and now I do not know of what I am capable. My head was filled with a lot of phantasies, but my heart was not as worn as I had feared; I say this now because I feel it. I felt it when I was in love with P. M. [Prosper Mérimée]. He rebuffed me and I must have recovered quickly; but now, far from being unhappy and misunderstood, I have found such candour, such loyalty, such tenderness that they intoxicate me. It is a young man's love and a comrade's friendship. It is something I never knew about, that I never thought of finding, and especially not in him. I would not believe in this affection, I repulsed it and at first refused it, but then I surrendered and am glad that I did so. I surrendered more out of friendship than love, and the love I did not know was revealed to me with none of the suffering that I had expected to have to accept.

I am happy, thank God for me. . . .

Now that I have told you what is in my heart, let me tell you what I am going to do. Planche has passed for my lover, I didn't care, and did not deny it. I only told my friends the truth: he was not. It is now very important to me that everyone should know that he is not, as much as it is unimportant that people should think that he was. You will understand that I cannot live in intimate relationship with two men who might seem to be on the same terms with me; that would not suit any of our natures.

I have therefore decided, very painfully but inevitably, to break with Planche. We discussed the matter frankly and affectionately and when we parted we shook hands on it, still deeply fond of one another. . . .

I do not know whether you will be pleased at my bold behaviour. You may perhaps think that a woman should hide her affections. But I would like you to understand that I am in a quite exceptional situation, and that I am obliged from now on to lead my private life in public. I do not pay much attention to public opinion; but if it is easy for me to enlighten it on the main points I must do so. I shall be said to be inconstant and self-willed, to have gone from Planche to Musset, until I go from Musset to someone else. No matter, so long as it is not said that I am sleeping with two men at one and the same time.

This letter expressed both George's new love for Alfred and her theories on sexual behaviour with equal frankness. Love was normal, necessary to her, and therefore good. She was never—throughout her life—lightly 'on with the new love, off with the old'. What had to be done was done, ruthlessly if need be. But solemnly, without a trace of humour or the least sense of the ridiculous, she stuck to her view that so long as she had only one lover at a time she was behaving both naturally and decorously. She showed no reluctance, either, to leading her private life in public.

On 19 September she wrote again to Sainte-Beuve:

I have been ill, but am now well. Besides, I am happy, very happy, my friend. Every day I am becoming more attached to *him*; every day I notice how small things that made me unhappy are vanishing; every day I see the lovely things about him that I admired, become brighter and more shining. And in addition to everything else, he is sweet-natured, and his nearness is as dear to me as his choice of me has been precious.

Living in this day-to-day and nightly intimacy, the lovers were getting to know one another. George found in Alfred what everyone else had found since his infancy, a sweetness of character that made him absolutely irresistible, an inexhaustible desire to please, serve, amuse and delight her. Gradually, however, she was to discover the darker side of that moon-silvery nature.

He also was to make discoveries. Already, in the letter in which he had declared his passion for her, a phrase rather odd in such a context had slipped in: 'There are a lot of things in your character that could have cured me. . . .' As they were now living together two of these characteristics soon began to affect his nerves.

The first was George's industry, for which, objectively, there could be nothing but praise. She wrote regularly, almost grimly, as professional writers must do in order to earn their living. Unfortunately she had formed the habit of working at night, sometimes throughout the night, a time usually reserved, especially with a new lover, for different exercises. Alfred not surprisingly found it extremely irritating when his mistress obliged him to postpone his ardent advances until she should have finished the next chapter, which had to be delivered to Buloz in the morning, or when, after Alfred was temporarily exhausted by their embraces, she even hopped out of bed in order to scribble away until dawn. '*Cette vache à écrire!*' he once called her in a moment of understandable temper.

He was still more exasperated by finding that although she obviously adored him and was wholly his, he could not arouse her senses. George herself had written in *Lélia* of the despair of a frigid woman, who, however much she longed to find physical satisfaction in love, for some mysterious reason could not do so. She had told herself that her own frigidity was due to the fact that she had never yet found her true mate, the man whose ardours and thrilling caresses would melt her whole body into surrender. No one could have been more deeply—greedily might not be an exaggerated term—

in love than George with Alfred during those first two months of their liaison, yet the ultimate satisfaction eluded her once again.

However much a lover may enjoy the possession of his mistress's body, however generously it may be surrendered to him (as George had with all her heart and soul surrendered hers) his satisfaction must be incomplete, clouded, if at the ultimate moment she is unable to share his physical ecstasy.

In Alfred's case this discovery was little short of disastrous. For he had acquired his physical experience mainly through lust, by sleeping with whores who had taught him the whole range and gamut of its expression. With this sexual experience and prowess he brought to George's bed deep, passionate and even pure love. Nevertheless he failed to make her share his sensations to the full.

Ever since his childhood, when his family had conspired to hide from him the marriage of his cousin, Clélie and during his adolescence, when the first woman whom he had loved had made a little fool of him, he had been convinced that women were natural deceivers. He could not accept the fact that George, who had already had several lovers, was simply frigid, incapable of fully satisfactory normal intercourse. In any case such a clinical psycho-physiological fact would hardly have been acceptable to his wildly romantic nature. It was therefore inevitable that he should become suspicious and seek the explanation elsewhere, in her past. Whom had she really loved before him? What had been her exact relationship with Casimir, her husband? On her marriage night? When she had been a virgin? And after Casimir had disgusted her by his coarseness and stupidity, had she really never had an affair with Aurélien de Sèze, her platonic lover? Then there was Jules Sandeau. . . . Everyone knew that Mérimée's attempt to conquer her had been a dismal, risible failure. Very well, but what other might perhaps have succeeded where he, Alfred, who adored her so passionately, appeared to fail?

George had nothing to hide nor did she wish to hide anything; she loved him as dearly as he loved her. And after the scenes he now began to make there were always tearful, tender reconciliations. These scenes were merely the 'little things' that made her suffer; and in her first letter to Sainte-Beuve she had expressed surprise that this new love had not, as yet, caused her suffering.

At the end of August they made several excursions to Fontainebleau and stayed there during September. They had aways been great walkers as well as talkers and adored the glorious woods and forests in the vicinity of Paris which are never more beautiful than in early autumn. George had promised Alfred that there she would tell him the whole story of her life; that he might question her down to the last detail and that she would answer faithfully, keeping nothing from him. So one moonlight night they set out for another walk in the forest and when they came to a clearing surrounded by great limestone rocks, George sat down on a boulder and began to speak.

The evidence for what occurred on this occasion rests, naturally, only on the stories afterwards told by Alfred and George themselves, since there were no other witnesses present. In 1835, Alfred was to write his version of their affair in his novel *La Confession d'un Enfant du Siècle*, in which George Sand appears under the name of Brigitte Pierson.

'Do not think,' she told him, 'that I do not understand your heart, or that I reproach you for making me suffer. It is not your fault that you have not the power to forget your own past; you have loved me deeply, and even if your love were to kill me, I would never regret having given myself to you. You thought that in my arms you would be re-born, and would forget those women who ruined you. I used to laugh, once, Octave, when you boasted of your precocious experiences, like a child that knows nothing . . . what did they do, to poison your youth? The pleasures they sold you must have been very powerful and dreadful, since you ask me to resemble them! You remember them when you are with me. Oh, my child, that is the most awful thing . . . to see on your face that frightful expression of libertine gaiety, which like some awful plaster mask slips in between your lips and my own. . . . Yet in spite of yourself your heart is noble; you blush for what you have done; you love me too much not to suffer when you see how I suffer . . . the first time

I saw you like that I was more terrified than I can tell you . . . I thought you were a mere roué . . . I wanted to die; what a night I spent! You do not know my life . . . you do not know that my experience has been no kinder than yours.

'You are not, my dear Octave, the first man whom I have loved.'

Whilst the above report of their conversation is almost certainly true, the *Confession* was written in the form of a novel, and the account the heroine, Brigitte, then gives her lover, Octave, of her unhappy marriage is obviously fictional as far as George was concerned. She tells him that she has had only one lover, but in the closing paragraphs of chapter three, one can almost hear George speaking:

'You told me in your better moods that Providence had charged me to watch over you like a mother. And that, my dear friend, is true. I am not always your mistress. Yes, when you make me suffer, I do not think of you as my lover, you are then nothing more to me than a sick child, defiant or sulky, whom I want to take care of or cure in order to find again the man I love and want always to love. . . .'

She burst into tears.

'Oh, my only friend!'—(he cried, as he took her into his arms)—'My mistress, my mother and my sister! Pray that I may love you as you deserve . . . that I may live, that my heart may be cleansed by your tears. . . .'
We sank down upon the stone. Around us all was silent; above us the sky was resplendent with stars. . . .
Thank God that since that evening we never went back to those rocks. The place became an altar, unsullied; one of the only spectres in my life that, when it rises before my eyes, is still pure white.

That was Alfred's account of the evening at the rocks of Franchard, written only two years after their visit there, when, filled with deep remorse and self-hatred, he painted his mistress as a saint and himself as an almost irreclaimable sinner. The words 'mother' and 'sister' again emphasize their pseudo-incestuous relationship. He was never to forget that hallowed spot, even returned there eight years later and afterwards wrote one of his greatest poems, *Souvenir*.

George's account of what happened at Fontainebleau was somewhat different and highly sensational. It was written in *Elle et Lui* twenty-six years later, after Alfred's death. According to her, when she had talked to him so kindly and maternally, he had suddenly experienced a violent brain-storm and rushed away from her into the depths of the forest, screaming. She tried to run after him, called him, but in vain. And when at dawn he returned to her, he told her that he had experienced a ghastly hallucination. He had seen a man, wild and dishevelled, who bore down on him as if about to attack him. As this apparition, which appeared to be pursued by the demons of hell, came closer, however, Alfred saw that he was in fact fleeing, seeking to escape, and as he rushed past he recognized in him his own features. He was his double or *Doppelgänger*.

Alfred's great poem, *La Nuit de Décembre*, written at the end of 1835, deals with this double of his. But as has already been pointed out this was not his own original concept or invention; it was a favourite theme of romantic poets. Moreover, when at the end of the poem the poet asks this phantom (who throughout has been presented as a sad, wistful, but in no wise terrifying figure) whence he comes, what he wants of him, and who, in fact, he is, the vision replies:

> Le ciel m'a confié ton coeur.
> Quand tu seras dans la douleur,
> Viens à moi sans inquiétude.
> Je te suivrai sur le chemin;
> Mais je ne puis toucher ta main,
> Ami, je suis la solitude.

> Heav'n gave your heart into my care.
> When pain and sorrow are your share
> Come to me then, without distress.

I'll follow closely in your wake,
Although your hand I may not take,
My friend, for I am Loneliness.

Solitude—and nothing worse or more sinister was, according
to Alfred, his life-long companion. And of what poet or other
inspired, creative genius would the same not be true?

2

Whether or not Alfred's neurotic or possibly hysterical
behaviour had frightened George, it did not apparently cause
her love for him to wane at this stage, nor did it deter her from
going on living with him. They now planned to visit Italy
together. Alfred was still resident at home. Although the
Revue des deux Mondes published everything he wrote he was
not earning sufficient to be financially independent, nor would
his mother have wished that he should live elsewhere than
with her, however much time he spent with his mistress.
Madame Edmée de Musset's feelings about Alfred's liaison
with the notorious Madame Sand were probably mixed. No
doubt any steady relationship with an older woman seemed
to her preferable to his former associations with women
of easy virtue, of which by then she may have had some
inkling. Madame Sand was an eccentric, whose private life
was already notorious. Yet she was also recognized as a woman
of genius by Alfred's colleagues on the *Revue des deux Mondes*.
And Madame de Musset, convinced since his babyhood of
her son's genius, could not remain unimpressed by that fact.
In France it was always much more usual than in England to
regard genius as a heaven-sent benefaction, whatever draw-
backs in the way of weakness—either of health or moral
standards—it might also confer. The two ladies had, naturally,
not met but Alfred's mother was probably as curious about
the woman who had inspired such passionate love in him as
most mothers of adored sons would have been.
    When, one day, however, he broached the subject of taking
a journey to Italy with Madame Sand, Madame de Musset
received the suggestion with the utmost disfavour. His health

came first; he was much too delicate to travel so far away and would certainly fall ill or even die:

> Alfred de Musset knew that he could not leave for Italy until he had received his mother's consent [Paul wrote in his *Biography*]. After our family luncheon one morning, he seemed preoccupied. As I was aware of his plans, I was hardly less agitated than he. When we rose from table he walked up and down, hesitatingly. Finally he plucked up courage and with many precautions informed us of his intentions, adding that, of course, they were subject to his mother's approval. His request was received as if he had told her of some great disaster. 'Never,' his mother answered, 'will I consent to a journey which might be dangerous and even fatal to you. I know that my opposition to it will be futile and that you will go, but it will be against my will and without my permission.'

> When Alfred attempted to argue the point with Madame de Musset she burst into tears, whereupon he immediately told her that he would give up the whole plan. 'Do not worry,' he said to his mother, 'I shall not go; if it is inevitable that someone should weep, it shall not be you.'
>
> Both Alfred and his mother, however, had someone else to reckon with, someone who was not used to being thwarted in her plans and who now decided on the measures to be taken in order to carry them out.
>
> At nine o'clock that same evening Madame de Musset was sitting by the fireside with her daughter, quietly reading when

> she was informed that a lady in a hackney carriage was waiting at the door for her and urgently wanted to speak to her. . . . She went downstairs. The unknown lady introduced herself; she begged the distressed mother to trust her son to her, saying that she would care for him with maternal affection. Promises were insufficient; she swore to do so. She summoned up all her eloquence and no doubt it must have been considerable, for she won her way.

And [Paul added] in spite of
mother who remained to weep

On the evening of December
travellers to their coach. George v
the journey—a black velvet jack
trousers and high leather boots, a
In her left hand she carried a stri
in her right, a bottle of champag
noted that their coach was the thi
And when it started it hit a post an
carrier.

They took a steamship down t
fellow-passengers was the French consul in Civita-Vecchia,
M. Henri Beyle, known to posterity as Stendhal. He was
apparently drunk most of the time and made cynical fun of
the romantic Madame Sand's idealizations of Italy and the
Italians. She loathed him at sight and gave a sigh of relief
when they parted company. But M. Beyle and M. de Musset
had a great deal in common. They were both writers of genius
and admired one another. Alfred's high spirits at the beginning
of this trip expressed themselves in cartoons and caricatures,
the most merciless of which was a self-portrait and the funniest
a drawing of Stendhal dancing. George was spared his malice;
all her portraits emphasize the beauty of her black eyes and
hair, the grace of her neck and hands, the charm of her
movements. In one of this series she is imperturbably smoking
a cigarette on board their ship from Marseille to Genoa, whilst
her romantic but self-mocking lover is being violently sea-sick.

﹥﹥﹥ V ﹤﹤﹤

Venetian triangle

I

THE LIGHT, the colour, the wines, the luscious dark Italian
beauties, seemed to Alfred to promise the very heights of
pleasure. When they arrived in Genoa he was just twenty-
three, a dangerous age for an impressionable youth to be for
the first time enthralled by such a sun, so warmly welcomed.
Almost from the moment they landed, he soaked himself in
this joyous atmosphere, at first as decorously as any tourist.
He went sight-seeing, mostly alone.

George had obtained the necessary subsidy for this trip
from Buloz—an advance of four thousand francs on her next
novel which he was to serialize. As conscientiously as usual she
shut herself up in her hotel room to write her daily stint. After
spending a few days in Genoa they went on to Florence.

Alfred was enchanted by this glorious city. He also
remembered there that Florentine blood ran in his own
veins. One of his remoter ancestors was a Salviati, a member
of the famous family whose fortunes had been bound up with
hose of the Medicis. Alfred was inspired both by his environment and this hereditary affinity to write a play, a dramatic
version of the murder of Duke Alexander de Medici by his
cousin, Lorenzino, in 1537. The play was entitled *Lorenzaccio*.
At the end of this play, in a few significant lines, the romantic
ruffian who was its hero tells his friend, Philippe Strozzi:

LORENZO: I was an instrument of murder, but of only one
    murder.
PHILIPPE: Could you not have been happy save by com-
    mitting murder? . . . Why should you wish to die?

75

LORENZO: I can only repeat, Philippe, that I have been honest. Perhaps I could become so again, were it not for the boredom I suffer. I still like wine and women; that is enough for me to be debauched, but it is not enough to make me want to be so.

The conflict in his hero's mind seems to reflect a similar condition in the author's. Alfred was, of course, still madly in love with George. He made some delightful sketches of her. When she took time off from writing they visited the galleries and museums together. Unfortunately, although she, too, was as much in love with him as ever, her amorous technique had not improved.

Florence, however, was no city in which to be bored or in which there was any lack of alcholic stimulation, of heady wines, or of erotic attractions. Alfred had too much time to spare. In spite of the romantic vows and tears of Fontainebleau he soon began to revert to those baser pleasures that he had in all sincerity resolved to renounce. To George it was a bitter disappointment to find him so quickly relapsing into those vicious habits of which his undoubted love for her should by this time have cured him. Her own conscience was now involved in their conflict as well, for she had sworn to his mother to watch over him with maternal vigilance. Her increasingly maternal attitude, however, only had the effect of stimulating Alfred's irrepressible urge to behave like a naughty child. ('I can embrace a foul and dead-drunk prostitute, but I cannot embrace my mother.') He had also begun to gamble again, and one night was obliged to confess to her that he had lost a fairly large sum in some brothel. The situation was aggravated by the fact that this trip was being financed by her labours. With that didactic logic of hers George unhesitatingly pointed out to him that the constant scribbling which so confoundedly irritated him was necessary to pay for his pleasures.

Yet their mutual recriminations did not come to a climax in Florence. Their quarrels were still followed by penitence on Alfred's part and forgiveness on George's. She may well have felt after a few weeks, however, that a change of scene had become highly desirable. Alfred himself was eager to see more of Italy. They agreed to move on and discussed their future plans with pleasant anticipation. Where should they go next? Their choice was almost evenly divided between Rome and Venice but they could not make up their minds which of these exciting cities to visit first. Finally, on Alfred's suggestion, they decided to toss for it. Ten times they spun the coin and ten times the answer was 'Venice'.

They arrived there at ten o'clock at night, on 19 January 1834. The weather was cold and depressing. In almost pitch darkness they embarked in a gondola, huddling under the hood for protection. Its strange elongated shape reminded them morbidly of a coffin; they might, as it slowly proceeded along the murky silent waters of the Grand Canal, have been dead souls crossing the Styx. This was their first and sinister impression of Venice. It was dispelled, however, when they parted the leather curtains that they had drawn to protect them from the wind and the water-mists. All along the Grand Canal the torchlight from the ancient palaces on its banks was glowingly reflected by the wavelets. To the gentle splashing of their gondolier's oar they were carried onwards towards the quay of the Schiavoni. A large dull red moon appeared above the square of St. Mark and silhouetted against the sky they beheld the exquisite traceries of the most fantastic cathedral in the world and the splendour of the Ducal Palace. Gliding past the Bridge of Sighs, their gondola finally tied up at the steps in front of Danieli's hotel.

> In Venice Tasso's echoes are no more,
> And silent rows the songless gondolier;
> Her palaces are crumbling to the shore,
> And music meets not always now the ear:
> Those days are gone—but Beauty still is here.
> States fall, arts fade—but Nature doth not die,
> Nor yet forget how Venice once was dear,
> The pleasant place of all festivity,
> The revel of the earth, the mask of Italy!

Alfred knew his 'Childe Harold'. He, too, like his beloved Byron, was enraptured by the glamour of 'the pearl of the Adriatic'. He wrote long, enthralled letters home:

When [wrote Paul] he found himself in the dying city of the Doges, he was as happy as a child. He considered that even his room at Danieli's hotel . . . was worth describing. He never wearied of studying those canopies beneath which in days gone by the head of some great Venetian family had strolled, or of observing from his window the view of the entrance to the Grand Canal and the dome of the Salute.

He began almost immediately to make notes on Venetian customs, on the dialect, and gossiped with the gondoliers, gathering local colour for the novel or play with a Venetian setting he resolved one day to write.

But poor George now had the worst imaginable luck. She had felt unwell ever since their arrival in Italy. Within a few days she was stricken by a violent attack of dysentery. Even had Alfred been a great deal older and much less romantic he might like any more prosaic lover on honeymoon with his beloved in the most magical city in the world, have found the situation frustrating and intensely depressing. Even had he been capable of coping with it, George would still not have wanted him to see her in this deplorable condition. There are ailments and diseases—such as tuberculosis—which sometimes confer added beauty and certainly pathos on their victims. But not dysentery. The wretched sufferer from it invariably feels involuntary shame and self-disgust and wants to hide away from all human contacts until the attack has passed. If the victim, as in her case, was a woman in love with a much younger, extremely sensitive and fastidious man, she would far prefer to die in solitude rather than let him see her in so miserable and unattractive a state. Willy-nilly, George was left for days and nights on end, suffering and scribbling the next instalment for Buloz when she was able to hold a pen. Alfred's absence may have been due to heartlessness but also to a tactful desire that she should not see in his face the sense of disgust which he was unable to conceal. For this view there is evidence in her own words, when she wrote to him, later: 'A sick woman is a very depressing and boring sight.' There seems little doubt that, however madly Alfred may have been in love with her before and after her

George Sand's eyes; background, George Sand at a window

Mon cher Georges, vos beaux yeux noirs que j'ai outragés hier, m'ont trotté dans la tête ce matin — je vous envoie cette ébauche, toute laide qu'elle est, par curiosité, pour voir si vos amis la reconnaitront, et si vous la reconnaitrez vous-même.

Good night — I am gloomy to day —

Alf^d de M^{tt}

(Bibliothèque Nationale)

Letter from Alfred de Musset to George Sand, enclosing drawing illness, he was completely out of love with her during that time.

But George's illness was almost as disastrous for Alfred as it was for her. It left him once again with unrestricted leisure in which to satisfy his unbridled appetites for the venal pleasures Venice had to offer. Venetian women had always had the reputation of being the most immoral as well as the most attractive in Italy. Byron had not only written exquisite verses on the beauty and history of that ambiguous city. Like him, Alfred now also plunged into its secretive alley-ways, the mysterious silent houses along the small canals, or *rios*, where brothels and gambling-dens and drink-shops abounded, offering excitement, adventure and debauchery. Unrestrainedly he drank, fornicated, played, returning at dawn to Danieli's and his suffering mistress's gloomy room, still drunk from the night's excesses, wild-eyed, depraved.

Floods of tears ensued but now it was George who wept, enough to have raised the water-level of the Grand Canal. Alfred was unrepentant, unkind, brutal. Poor Coelio had been completely ousted by his evil double, Octave. Never sober, he was bored to death by this drab, dreary, preaching female, who looked (as she was) several years older than himself, tyrannically maternal. This was not the good companion, the comrade, friend, fellow-traveller and lover with whom he had set out on a voyage of fun and adventure. There was no longer any use pretending. The affair had come to a dead end. Coldly, with that mean cynical glance that so deeply distressed her Alfred now informed her: 'George, I must beg your pardon. I do not love you. In fact, I never was in love with you.'

I never complained, [she wrote to him later,] I never hid my tears from you and those appalling words were spoken, on a certain evening I shall never forget, at Danieli's hotel. . . . The communicating door between our rooms was closed and we tried to take up once again our former relationship of two good comrades, but it was no longer possible. You were bored, I do not know what you did with yourself at night and one day you told me that you feared . . .

F

He had told her that he feared he might have caught a venereal disease from a trollop with whom he had spent the previous night in a brothel.

Those edifying letters referred to by Paul, which no doubt gave Madame de Musset great satisfaction and which seemed to have allayed the intuitive forebodings with which she had reluctantly given George her consent to Alfred's journey to Italy, abruptly ceased at the beginning of February. What had happened?

4 February [1834]
Read this when you are alone!

My dear Buloz, your reproaches have reached me at a sad time. Had you received my letter, you would know already that I do not deserve them. Well, for the past fort-night I had recovered and was working. Alfred, too, was working, although he was slightly unwell and had attacks of fever from time to time. About five days ago we both became ill, I, with dysentery which made me suffer horribly, and from which I have not yet recovered but which nevertheless now leaves me enough strength to nurse him; he, with an inflammatory nervous fever, which has developed rapidly to the point when, to-day, he is very ill and the doctor does not know what to think of it. We shall have to wait until the twelfth or thirteenth day to know whether or not his life is in danger! And what day will that twelfth or thirteenth be? His last, perhaps! I am desperate, worn out, suffering horribly, and expecting what kind of a future! . . . Alfred cannot be moved and possibly for another month, supposing all goes well. . . . If my misery lasts till the end and Alfred dies, I assure you that I shall not care what happens to me afterwards . . . I am sorry about the delay in sending you your copy. But is it my fault? If Alfred were to have a few quiet days I could finish my work very quickly. But he is in an appalling state of agitation and delirium. I cannot leave him for an instant, it has taken me nine hours to write you this letter.

Good-bye, my friend. Pity me.

George

Above all, on no account, do not tell anyone, anyone in this world, that Alfred is ill. If his mother heard of it, she would go mad. If she has to hear of such a disaster, it does not matter how, but if Alfred is out of danger in fifteen days, there is no point in alarming her at present. . . .

8 February 1834

George Sand to Boucoiran:

My child,
I am still greatly to be pitied. He is really in danger. . . . The nerves in the brain are so deeply affected that his delirium is dreadful and continuous. To-day, however, he is extraordinarily better. His reason has completely returned and he is perfectly calm. But last night was horrible. Six hours of such frenzy that in spite of two strong men, he was running around the room naked. He shouted, sang, screamed, had convulsions, oh my God, my God, what a sight! When he embraced me he nearly strangled me. The two men could not get him to let go of my collar. The doctors say he will have another similar attack to-night, and possibly still more, for we cannot be sure for another six days. Will he have enough strength to endure these horrible crises? Am I not unhappy enough, and you, who know my life, can you think of many worse? . . .
Fortunately I have found an excellent young doctor, who stays with him day and night and whose remedies seem to have a very good effect. . . ."

The name of the young doctor was Pietro Pagello.
On February 13 she wrote to Buloz that Alfred was saved. Her very long letter concerned her and Alfred's debts to him, her determination to repay them, both by work, and if need be, in cash. Meantime, she implored him to send her more money. In the midst of his delirium Alfred was worrying about his own debts, both to Buloz and to others. George assured Buloz that she would repay everything.

If only you knew, my friend, what that delirium was like! What sublime and appalling things he said . . . I do not know how I had the strength to endure, and how I did not go mad myself.

The cause of Alfred's sudden breakdown was never made clear. Malaria? Typhoid? But whether or not he was suffering from some infection or other that gave him a terrific temperature, his symptoms may also have been aggravated if they were not solely due to, an attack of delirium tremens, or alcoholic poisoning, the result of the violent debauchery in which he had indulged when George had closed that door between their rooms in the Hotel Danieli. They had moved before he fell ill because she could no longer afford to stay there. She had written to the new young doctor who had been recommended to her—Signor Pagello—from the Hotel Royal. In this letter she told him that although the patient was extremely weak and 'often talked like a child', he was in fact of strong character, with a powerful imagination, a poet greatly admired in France.

> Once, about three months ago, as the result of great mental strain, he was like a madman, for the whole of one night. He saw phantoms all around him, and screamed with fear and horror. . . . This morning, he knows neither what he is saying or doing. He weeps, complains of some indefinable pain, is homesick, and says that he will either die or go mad!
>
> I do not know whether this is the result of his fever, his nervous hypertension, or a form of madness. . . .
>
> He is the one being whom I love most in all the world and seeing him in this condition gives me great anguish. . . .

'Madman,' 'mad,' 'madness'—three times this suggestion recurs in this letter. There is no doubt at all that Alfred was far from normal. A very high temperature could cause even the best-balanced person to rave. Delirium is also one of the principal symptoms of alcoholic poisoning. Yet the phrase, ' I think I shall go mad' or 'I feel as if I were going mad' is often colloquially used by anyone suffering acute mental distress. This does not, however, make them mad, or certifiable, in a clinical sense.

Meantime, he was the one being whom she loved most in the world—for the next few days.

The moment Alfred fell desperately ill George did not forget but temporarily put aside all her grievances against him, a treasure of bitterness on which she would freely draw as soon as she found it necessary to justify her own subsequent conduct. She was, moreover, an impeccable nurse. On 13 February she wrote to Buloz:

> My friend, Alfred is saved, he has not had another crisis and it is now nearly the fourteenth day that there has been no relapse. . . . At present he is in a state of extreme weakness . . . needing constant nursing day and night . . . . I have not undressed for eight nights, I sleep on a sofa and am up every hour. . . ."

And she informed Buloz that as soon as he was better, she intended to bring Alfred back to Paris. Matters did not, however, work out that way.

There was no doubt that in addition to George's devoted nursing Alfred owed his life to the clever young doctor whom she had called in.

Dr. Pagello, in spite of his Italian name, was blond, rosy-cheeked, blue-eyed, slightly plump and probably of Tyrolese ancestry. Although he had not been long in practice his lack of experience was outweighed by his undoubted medical ability, reinforced by an amiable and calm nature. No greater contrast could have been conceived even in George's fertile novelist's brain, than between the delicate febrile patient, and the robust steady-nerved doctor.

To Pagello, the nurse must have seemed almost as romantic and pathetic as the patient. How fantastic they were, this French pair—the sick poet and his mistress, with her enormous tragic black eyes, her terrible responsibility for this unfortunate boy, who might at any moment die far away from home, from that mother to whom his companion had so faithfully promised to bring him back, happy and well. It was not altogether professional conscientiousness that kept Pagello almost as permanently by Alfred's bedside as George. He had already had a fair amount of amorous success; he had a steady liaison with a Venetian mistress and there was no lack of other women in his own city who found him attractive. Yet he now gave up his leisure as well, ignoring all his engagements in order to spend hours at a time, day and night, in Alfred's room or, with George, in the adjoining one.

It is improbable that it ever occurred to him to attempt to seduce this exotic creature who had implored him to save the life of the one being whom she loved most in all the world. How could he have imagined—and he was certainly not an imaginative man—that within a few days 'La Sand' (as he thought of her) would transfer the whole weight of her over-whelming passion to so insignificant a recruit as himself? How, indeed, could anyone have imagined such a situation, that even the most romantic or fantastic novelist would not have dared to invent?

Whenever possible George scribbled a few pages of the novel she owed to Buloz, against which she had been imploring him for further advances. So that when one evening Pagello saw her, as usual, writing page after page in precipitous haste he thought nothing of it. She suddenly folded up the closely written pages and handed them to him across the bed on which Alfred, still terribly weak but at last out of danger, lay sleeping. Pagello simply stood and stared, uncomprehending, and made no move to take them from her hand. After a moment George withdrew it and on the back of the sheets wrote, in enormous letters, TO STUPID PAGELLO. Then she handed them back to him and this time Pietro took them. He left without reading them. His expression when, at home, he did open what appeared to be an impassioned love-letter, must have been one of amazement, incredulity, and finally, gratification:

. . . How do you love? The passion of your glances, the violence of your embraces, the audacity of your desires, tempt and frighten me. I watch you with surprise, desire, anxiety; I do not know if you really love me; I shall never know. . . . My feeble nature and your fiery temperament must give birth to very different ideas. . . . Will you be my support or my master? What lies behind that virile chest, that lion's eye, that superb forehead? . . . Your eyes in which I seem to see divine lightnings. . . . When your mistress falls asleep in your arms, do you remain awake, watching her, praying to God and weeping? Do the pleasures of love leave you panting and exhausted, or filled with divine ecstasy? Does your soul depart from your body when you leave the one you love? You, at least, will not deceive me; you will make me no vain promises and false vows; you will love me as you know how and as you can. . . .

It was not only Alfred, clearly, whose mind and body had been poisoned by the miasmas of Venice. The significant thing about this effusion, however, is that it is almost an echo of Alfred's own romantic approach to love. George's style seems almost like a parody of his; the question-marks at the end of the sentences are hers. But we know from Alfred's *Confession* how often he had remained awake, watching her, praying and weeping for his sins:

'My friend, I told her from my very heart, I am deeply unhappy for having reproached you unjustly for a little innocent badinage; but if you love me, never lie to me about the smallest thing; to me lying is horrible and I cannot bear it.'
She went to sleep; it was three o'clock in the morning, and I told myself that I wanted to stay until she was asleep. I watched her close her lovely eyes . . . I kissed her good-night. I left with a quiet heart. . . .
But the sufferings I had endured, the memory of the treacheries I had witnessed, the corrupt world in which I had lived . . . and finally, debauchery, contempt for love . . . that was what lay in my heart although I did not yet know it; and at the moment when I thought to be reborn to hope and life, all those latent furies took me by the throat. . . .

Those lines were written a little later but were truthful and expressive of Alfred's emotions at an earlier date. Sand must often have awakened to find him beside her, adoring and self-reproachful, and not even when she wrote this first letter to Pagello could she have imagined him in a similar state of emotional conflict. During Alfred's illness she had been nursing her grudge, as well as him. 'You, at least, will not deceive me,' she told Pagello, 'you will make me no vain promises and false vows.' He never did. There was no emotional tension in Pietro. Like any other straightforward young man he took without complication what she offered him: her body. . . . He temporarily but nevertheless with slightly guilty qualms deserted his mistress and became George's lover.

She continued—although they were now sleeping together in the room next to Alfred's—to write him enormous letters in a similar strain:

> . . . You are young and strong, your soul is all new, all lovely, all vigorous. Well, even if you were only a brave and noble fool, you would be worth more than all those who deny. Take me where you will. I trust in your virtue; let us love, suffer and die together. . . .

This last sentence is also Musset, not Sand. For it was Alfred, not George, who had always equated love with suffering.

Pagello did not apparently find her sexually frigid at that time. He did find her glamorous and exciting. Although in her first declaration George had clearly wanted him to be her master, his relationship with her soon fell into the pattern she invariably imposed on all her lovers; he became a mere instrument in her own peculiar design for living.

Many conjectures were subsequently made as to George's reasons for her seduction of Dr. Pagello. She herself advanced several different theories to explain her motives, which varied from self-accusation to self-justification, according to time, place and circumstances. In fact it seems to have been due to two main motives. The first was plain lechery. Her nerves were exacerbated and needed a sedative; a young healthy lover was there to provide it. But emotionally she was, although she at that time refused to admit it to herself, still completely swayed by her passion for Alfred. His recent rebuttal of her, his brutally cold statement that he was not and never had been in love with her, had given her vanity a wound that was to bleed for a very long time. It was in the hope of staunching that wound that she had taken Pagello. In their terrible scene just before his illness Alfred had made it dreadfully clear that he regarded her no longer as young, beautiful, or bed-worthy. This affront had to be avenged.

She had to convince herself that he was wrong (as she would shortly do), before she proved it to him, or else there would have been no point in taking Pagello for her lover.

But first, with her phenomenal powers of rationalization, she had to persuade herself that she was completely in her rights in acting as she did. This was not difficult. When she had written to Sainte-Beuve explaining her dismissal of Planche, she had stated her moral principle: She was perfectly entitled to have one lover at a time but would have regarded it as indecent to have had two. Well, had she not closed the com-municating door between their rooms, on the night when Alfred had said he no longer and never had loved her? With that gesture she had (according to her theory) terminated the affair. From that moment onwards she was free to take another lover. In order to satisfy her requirements she had to build up those ridiculous myths about the simple Pagello—the lion-hearted male with a superb forehead. It was necessary to her self-respect that she should believe them. Poor Alfred! Poor sick boy! As he lay there, helpless, weak, very slowly convalescing, she racked her brains for the kindest, gentlest phrases in which to inform him, when once again he would be well, that he had been superseded. Without any sense of guilt or cruelty, without any conscious desire for revenge, she wrote to Pagello:

> Poor young poet, full of good intentions, but without the strength to carry them out! He is worthy of compassion, for he is full of a sense of guilt, and when he is alone and abandoned he has no refuge in his own conscience. He cannot, like you my friend, console himself by the memory of having done his duty, or a good deed; he gives way to all his bad impulses and suffers for it: we must pity him. . . . But there are the two of us to watch over him. Help me to accomplish this task until the end. We shall be so happy when, intoxicated by love, we will again be in one another's arms and be able to tell each other that we have nothing to blame ourselves for. . . .

This letter was written when Alfred was already a great deal better. In the meantime, however, Pagello, who was incapable of George's degree of self-deception, had been worrying about the possible outcome of the affair, once Alfred was well enough to be informed of La Sand's new attachment. In spite of their intrigue he was a conscientious doctor. Moreover, in addition to being now the accredited lover of Alfred's former mistress, he had developed a real and sincere affection for the sick young man whose life he had saved. He was afraid that the shock of hearing the news too soon might bring on a relapse. He suggested they should wait another month:

> ... Can we be sufficiently prudent and happy, you and I [George wrote to Pagello in reply to this suggestion], to hide our secret from him for a month? Lovers are impatient and cannot dissimulate. If I had taken a room at an inn we could have met without fearing that he would break into a fury from one moment to the next. ...

She knew herself and she knew her Alfred. As soon as he began to recover, his suspicions were aroused. In spite of what he had said to her in a moment of flaming temper he did still love her and with him love was always inseparable from jealousy. Moreover, he knew her tendency to promiscuity— or with reluctance suspected it. It seemed to him that between bouts of fever, as they bent over him or moved around the room, he had seen their amorous glances, the furtive contacts of their hands and that once they had even kissed one another, thinking him asleep.

Originally, George had intended to take him back to Paris as soon as he was able to travel but now she had to find some means of sending him home alone. For she was determined to remain in Venice with Pagello.

One morning Alfred, now convalescent, went into George's adjacent room. On a table he saw there a tray with a tea-service which had not been cleared away since the previous night. There was only one cup and saucer.

'So you had tea yesterday evening?' he said to George.

'Yes,' she replied, 'I had tea with the doctor.'

'Oh?' Alfred appeared to be puzzled, 'but there's only one cup.'

'I suppose,' she shrugged, 'the other one was cleared away.'

'Oh no,' Alfred countered, 'nothing has been cleared away. The fact is, you both drank from the same cup.'

'And supposing we did?' George snapped back, 'you no longer have any right to question me about things like that.'

'As I still pass for your lover, I have the right. You might at least have that much respect for me and wait three days, until I've left.'

As soon as he was able to go out, he went to a drinking-shop and became drunk on the heavy wine of Cyprus they sold there. What Pagello had feared came to pass; more fever, more delirium. But he was certain that his suspicions about the tea-cup were correct. That same night he again went into George's room; she lay on her bed, writing.

'What are you doing?' asked Alfred.

'I'm reading,' but as she answered she blew out the candle.

'If you're reading, why blow out the candle?'

'It went out by itself; light it again.' He did so.

'Ah,' he accused her, 'you said you were reading, but you haven't a book. Why don't you admit that you were writing to your lover?'

Thereupon George began to weep, lament, moaning that she wished she were dead.

'All right,' Alfred crazily jealous, mocked her. 'Kill yourself! Take poison or throw yourself in the canal!'

He looked so wild, so desperate as he spoke, that George was genuinely frightened.

'He's mad!' she moaned, and rushed to the door. Alfred got there first, stood with his back to it and pushed her away. That word, which expressed aloud his own secret terrors, must have seemed to them both at that terrible moment perilously near the truth.

'I know your horrible plan,' he shouted at her. 'You're intending to rush to your doctor, have him certify me insane on the pretext that I tried to kill you. If you dare to try to go out, I shall fix such an epitaph on your tombstone that those who read it will turn pale.'

George dissolved into tears and complained that she was feeling ill; their appalling scene had given her violent internal pains.

Neither of them were to forget it for the rest of their lives.

But Alfred did not yet know the worst, the whole truth that he had indeed suspected, but of which he had no actual proof. He did not know for certain (nor for a long time afterwards) whether or not Pagello had become George's lover in the full sense of the term before this scene. When he had recovered from it he was as usual full of remorse for his cruelty and brutality towards her. Coelio reappeared in place of Octave. He loved her, still loved her more than ever and begged her forgiveness in abject repentance.

George now rose fully to the situation. She pointed out so gently, with such sweet reasonableness, what angelic devotion she had shown him during his illness. Alfred more than agreed with her, his gratitude was so deep that he could find no words for it. But, George continued, even her unremitting care would not have saved him had not that brilliant young doctor Pagello taken up his case. He too had spent days and nights by Alfred's bedside, never sparing himself, neglecting his other patients, his own private interests, until he had pulled him through. With this, too, he wholeheartedly agreed.

Alfred said this evening [George wrote to Pagello] what a man he is, that Pagello! What a good heart he has! What strength! It seems to me that compared to both of you, I am a dwarf. I am ashamed of myself. I feel that I should place your hand in his, and go away, weeping for the happiness that I did not know how to deserve. Pagello was the man for you, my poor George: he would have known how to respect you. . . .

One cannot help wondering whether those enormous dark eyes of George's had not some hypnotic quality. For, whether or not those were Alfred's actual words this was what she gradually led him to believe. The most important point in gaining her end, however, was that he should never suspect that she had begun her affair with Pagello two months previously:

> He would never let me go away with a man who had been my lover two months ago. . . .

When George saw that Alfred was sufficiently softened up to be moulded to the point to which she had all along intended to bring him, she spoke to him, still in the tenderest terms, of what had happened before his illness. It had been he who had first broken off their liaison; he who had told her that he did not love her, never had been in love with her. Finding herself thus rejected by him she had in her despair and loneliness, in spite of herself, to her own astonishment, fallen in love with Pagello. Had not Alfred himself declared that the strong, noble young doctor was the right man to make her happy?

He admitted that he had, and that her happiness was the only thing in the world that mattered to him. How could he, miserable weak wretch that he was, stand in her path? There was one good thing still left for him to do to atone for his sins against her. He would voluntarily and formally renounce George to Pietro.

On March 28 he told George to ask Pagello to come to them. When he arrived Alfred, sweet, calm, reasonable and completely sober, informed him that George had confessed that she loved him. He, Alfred, was prepared to sacrifice his own happiness to theirs. All he wanted was Pagello's assurance that he, too, loved George, and that he would care for and cherish her.

'You love one another,' he told Pagello with charming simplicity, 'and yet you both love me, as well; you have saved my life and my soul.'

Sublime moment!

On this occasion, George's description was perhaps not an overstatement. Alfred's generosity and sincerity were no doubt a shade theatrical; the scene smacks of the theatre. But he was a dramatist and whether or not he consciously or subconsciously enjoyed acting the hero in his own living drama of self-abnegation, the fact remains that there was not a grain of pretence in his action. He bore his love and his suffering like a gentleman, almost like a hero.

From that moment onwards all George's maternal comradely affection was again his. Not with indecent haste but punctiliously and devotedly she made all the necessary preparations to send him home, alone, to France and his mother. He was still weak, he would need a valet to look after him on the journey. She packed for him, booked his seat, and wrote him the tenderest of farewell letters. Alfred sent her a note from Padua, the first stop on his journey, as he had promised:

> You told me to leave and I have left; you told me to live, and I live. We stopped at Padua; it was eight o'clock at night and I was tired. Do not doubt my courage. Write me a line to Milan, dear brother, beloved George.

Her reply ran to many lines, as usual, for George could never express herself in fewer than several thousand words at a time:

> . . . I shall have no peace until this evening, and then what peace! Such a long journey, and you are still so weak! My God, My God! I shall pray to God from morning till night. I hope that He will hear me. . . . Do not worry about me. I am as strong as a horse, but do not tell me to be gay and tranquil. . . . Poor angel, how will you pass this night? I hope that you will have been tired enough to sleep. Be sensible and careful and good, as you promised me. . . .
>
> Good-bye, good-bye, my angel. . . . Ah, who will look after you now, and whom will I look after? Who will need me, and whom will I take care of . . . ?

This rhetorical question was to be answered a few years later. The name of the answer was Frédéric Chopin, whose genius was equal to Alfred's, whose health was equally delicate, and who was in his turn to be discarded when the time was ripe. In the meantime fate was reserving another ironical twist in George's and Alfred's relationship.

From Geneva Alfred replied to George, at almost equal length. His letter, nearly as long as hers, was pure 'Coelio':

> My dearest George, I am in Geneva. . . . Write to me in Paris, my dear friend, I left you very tired, very worn out by those two months of sadness, as you told me; you have a lot to tell me. Tell me, above all, that you are happy. . . . I am strong, well, almost happy. Should I say that I have not suffered, that in those sad nights in hotels I did not often weep? That would mean that I was a brute, and you would not believe me.
>
> I am still in love with you, George; with three hundred miles between us in the last four days, why should I not speak frankly? At such a distance there can be no more violent emotion or nervous crises; I love you, I know that you are with a man whom you love. I am quiet . . . it is no longer a worn-out child who is writing to you . . . I did not want to write until I was sure of myself; so many things went on in my poor head! From what strange dream have I awakened! This morning . . . I saw myself in a mirror, I recognized the child of past times. What did you do, my poor friend? Was that the man whom you wanted to love? You had ten years of suffering in your heart, since ten years you had had an inextinguishable thirst for happiness, and that was the reed on whom you wanted to lean! You, love me! My poor George! It made me tremble. I made you so unhappy, and what further terrible unhappiness had I not been on the point of causing you! I shall see it for a long time, my George, your pale face, watching eighteen nights over my bed; I shall see you for a long time in that sinister room where so many tears flowed! Poor George! Poor dear child! you were mistaken; you thought that you were my mistress, but you were only my mother. . . . It was incest that we were committing. . . .

The letter continued for many more pages in this self-deprecatory, sincere and noble strain. It was himself Coelio blamed, himself alone. Both of them were convinced the affair was over. Although he was still in love with her he accepted her now, completely, as his friend, his mother. It was wonderful,

perfect. To be in love with but no longer in circumstances
that made it possible for him to go to bed with 'his mother'.
The letter was written in pure ecstasy. Catharsis was
complete.

But the recipient was less satisfied. On April 15 she replied
with another enormous letter, an impassioned love-letter if
ever there was one:

> . . . Whether I was your mistress or your mother, what
> does it matter? I know that I love you and that is all. . . .
> To watch over you, keep you from all harm or annoyance,
> to provide you with amusement and pleasure, that is the
> need that I feel and regret since I lost you. . . . Why should
> I, who would have given my own blood to give you a night of
> repose and calm, have become a torment, a calamity, a
> spectre to you? When those awful memories assail me (and
> when do they leave me in peace?) I nearly go mad. I
> cover my pillow in tears. I hear your voice calling me in the
> silence of the night. Who is there now to call me? Who will
> need me to watch over him? How can I use the strength
> I stored up for you, and which now is turning against
> myself. . . ?

Remorse, guilt-feelings, masochistic rationalization; the letter
and those that followed during the next months go on in this
strain for pages and pages, so that it seems amazing that
George should still have found the time and energy to scribble as
well the instalments of her novel, and her *Lettres d'Un Voyageur*
for publication in the *Revue des deux Mondes*. But when her
emotions left her tear-ducts dry there were invariably practical
orders, instructions and directions at the end of these missives,
some of them detailed and precise. For George was also using
the devoted Alfred as her courier:

> Here are the little things I would ask you to send me.
> Twelve pairs of glacé gloves, two pairs of black satin slippers,
> and two pairs of black marocain, from Michiels at the
> corner of the Rue du Helder and the boulevard, tell him
> to make them a little bigger than my usual measurements,
> my feet are swollen and the Venetian marocain is as

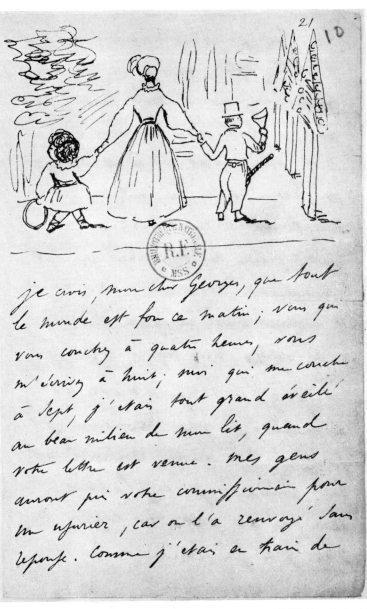

Letter headed by a drawing of George and her children

Portrait of George Sand by Delacroix

tough as buffalo hide, a quarter of patchouly from Leblanc, rue Sainte-Antoine, opposite No. 50—don't let yourself be rooked, it's worth 2 francs a quarter; Marquis sells it for six francs. . . .

He was also to see her son, Maurice, and send her detailed news of him. Alfred carried out all these commissions and instructions loyally and faithfully, as well as seeing Buloz on her behalf and countering, as well as reporting to her, the gossip that was running all around Paris as to the causes of their separation.

And the lion-eyed Pagello?

In August 1834, unable to endure her separation from Alfred any longer, having extracted from Venice all the copy she needed, bored and homesick, George arrived in Paris, bringing Pietro with her.

⁂⁂⁂ VI ⧉⧉⧉

Return of the penitent

I

'I SHALL bring home to you,' Alfred had warned his family, 'a sick body, a sorrowing soul and a bleeding heart, which, however, still loves you.'

He also brought back with him a prescription which he told them was for some strong sedative drug. 'It's a powerful narcotic and bitter, like everything else I owe to that man, even my life.' The prescription was signed: Pagello.

He begged them to give him a different room from his own. 'The thought of waking up and seeing that ugly bright green wallpaper will make me think that my four walls are covered with boredom and sadness.'

Paul immediately changed rooms with him. He arrived home on 10 April, accompanied by Antonio, who, however, was sent back to Venice when it was found that his presence only aggravated Alfred's depression. His family was, naturally, appalled at his condition, his pallor and thinness, but received him with the utmost love and thankfulness, careful never to utter a single reproach. When Alfred tried to tell them about his illness and the reasons for his returning alone to Paris he fainted dead away. He wrote his own recollections of those months five years later, in an unfinished autobiography, *Le Poète Déchu*:

At first I felt neither regret nor pain at my abandonment. I left proudly; but I had hardly looked around me when I beheld a desert. . . . It seemed as if all my thoughts were falling like dry leaves. . . . When I found that I could not struggle against it, I gave way in despair to my sorrow . . . I shut myself away in my room; and there I spent four

months . . . seeing no one and for my only distraction a
game of chess I played mechanically every evening. . . .
My sorrow gradually grew calmer, my tears dried up, my
insomnia passed away.

He burned all his former favourite books and pictures;
none of them meant anything more to him.

I knew then the meaning of experience and I saw that
suffering teaches us the truth. . . .
My mistress was dark; she had large eyes; I loved her,
she had left me; I had suffered and wept for four months;
was not that enough?

He was unable to write a line of verse but after a time he did
manage to produce a short play which was published in the
Revue des deux Mondes under the title: *On ne badine pas avec l'amour*.
This was to become one of his most famous pieces. He had
begun to write it in verse before leaving for Venice with
George. But on his return he re-wrote it in prose. Perdican, the
hero, courts the proud and lovely Camille and at the same time
banteringly makes love to the innocent Rosette, daughter of
Camille's wet-nurse, who has been brought up with her.
Camille and Perdican finally confess their mutual passion to
one another and decide to marry. But suddenly the curtain
falls on tragedy. Rosette, having overheard their decision, kills
herself for love of Perdican. Camille thereupon leaves him and
so he loses both his 'sacred' and 'profane' loves. Moral: It is as
dangerous to play with love as with fire.
The sudden switch of this light-hearted pastoral comedy
into moving tragedy is one of Alfred's most successful and
touching *coups de théâtre*.
Buloz was extremely sympathetic towards Alfred. Most of
George's colleagues took an unfavourable view of her behaviour.
Knowing Alfred's weaknesses as they did, it still seemed to
them almost incomprehensible and even slightly scandalous
that she should have taken his doctor as her new lover and sent
him home, weak and miserable, only just twenty-four, too
young to bear such an experience even had he been strong
and healthy.

Paul and Alfred Tattet, Alfred's most intimate friend, were also implacable in their condemnation of George. When he grew a little stronger and able to talk about his heart-break, they spent hours, whole days and nights with him. But neither his colleagues on the *Revue des deux Mondes*, neither his friend nor his brother, could bring him to speak one word against George:

> Alfred got wind of some of the gossip that was going around [wrote Paul] and never spared himself in his denials of everything that could harm the person he had left in Venice. In that he was only doing his duty as a gentleman; but he was unable to hide his sadness or the change in his expression and the malevolent guesses went on in spite of him.
>
> As for those who had taken away his peace of mind, it was not enough for him to have forgiven them; he tried to find excuses for them, or at least extenuating circumstances, so much did he fear that the post would bring him no more letters from Venice! He wrote, himself, always taking the blame for what had happened; some of his letters contained verses.

This was in fact his chief occupation and preoccupation during the spring and summer of 1834—this enormous corre-pondence he was carrying on with George. His angel, his beloved, his darling Georgeot, were the terms in which he addressed her. One of the most important of these letters was dated 1 May 1834:

> Do you know why I love you alone? . . . I do not hide any of your faults from myself; you do not lie, that is why I love you. I remember that night of the letter very well . . . [the night she had blown out the candle when he had caught her writing a love-letter to Pagello]. But tell me, if all my suspicions had been justified, in what were you deceiving me? Did you tell me that you loved me? Had I not been warned? Had I any rights . . . ? Oh, my darling child, when you loved me did you ever deceive me . . . ? Lying is what I abhor, what makes me the most

defiant of men, perhaps the unhappiest. But you are as
sincere as you are noble and proud. . . .

These phrases sound a little ambiguous. Was Alfred
whistling to keep his courage up? Was he hoping for some
further admission from George about her relations with
Pagello during his illness, before he had given them his blessing?
Had it occurred to him that they had been lovers before that
'sublime' night, so precious to all three of them? It seems
unlikely that at this stage he doubted George's honesty and
sincerity. If he did, he was straining every nerve to repress
such doubts, to see his beloved as nothing less than a pure and
shining angel. A little later followed this paragraph:

> Tell Pagello that I thank him for loving and looking
> after you as he is doing. Is that sentiment not the most
> ridiculous thing in the world? I love that boy almost as
> much as you do; sort it out as you like. Through him my
> life has lost all its riches and I love him as if he had given
> them to me. I would not like to see you together and yet
> I am happy to think that you are together. Oh, my angel,
> my angel, be happy and I will be so, too.

Self-immolation or masochism? But whether or not he
had persuaded himself as to George's right to act as she had,
he was determined to take her side against himself. Coelio
could not forgive Octave for his cruelty to his beloved. (Nor
could George forgive herself for what she was already realizing
was her own stupidity. It was becoming clearer to her every
day that she had exchanged an infuriating but adorable and
adoring genius for a kind, good-natured, decent, honest bore.)
The most important passage in this letter is the following:

> I am going to write a novel. I very much want to write
> our story. I feel that it would heal me and lift up my heart.
> I would like to build you an altar, were it with my own
> bones. . . .

The novel was written. It was entitled *La Confession d'un
Enfant du Siècle*. It was Alfred's only long novel, and was

published on 1 February 1836. The plot is thin. The narrator, Octave, has two mistresses. The first, unnamed, is portrayed as a cynical siren, the second, Brigitte Pierson, as an angel. The main personal theme is the situation that develops between Octave, Brigitte, and Smith, the honest Englishman to whom in the end Octave loses her. It is an exact parallel to the Alfred-George-Pagello situation. Alfred-Octave unequivocally attributes his loss of Brigitte-George to his own weaknesses, alcoholism and lust, from which she had in vain tried to save him.

The importance of this book, the reason why it has become a classic which still has validity in our own time, is to be found in its generalizations. For Alfred claimed to have written it as a warning to his contemporaries, his own generation, the sons of Napoleon's heroes, born of parents weakened and worn out by the stress of battle. The magnificent opening lines have passed into most anthologies of French prose. This theme remains topical so long as war remains. After the Second World War every country produced its quota of restless, unhappy youths, unsettled to an even greater degree than Alfred de Musset and many of his contemporaries. They, too, had their 'dandyism'; their need for re-assurance compelled them to wear almost exactly the same kind of exaggerated costume as his did—the long, flamboyant jackets, the tight trousers, the bright colours. Although the tall hat no longer figures in their apparel, their hair-cuts are closely similar to the sweeping locks and side-burns worn by Alfred in the medallion by David d'Angers, sculpted when he was twenty. These psychologically unstable children of our own century also sought self-annihilation in drugs and alcohol and mutual annihilation in gang-fights, their flick-knives always at the ready.

La Confession d'un Enfant du Siècle remains an historical and sociological document, as valid today as when it was written. It is also indispensable as a key to Alfred's personal experience. For although he later attempted to deny that it was auto-biographical, it was more so than anything else he wrote. In the description of the scene between Octave and Brigitte at the rocks of Franchard in the forest of Fontainebleau he gave his own version of what happened between himself and George on a similar occasion. Had he not written it we would have no

RETURN OF THE PENITENT   101

evidence to place against George's prejudiced and exaggerated account of this incident in *Elle et Lui*.

2

Alfred could not bring himself to write to Pagello. But on 15 June Pietro sent him an affectionate note, from a friend and a medical adviser:

Venice, 15 June 1834

We have not yet written to one another, perhaps because neither of us wanted to be the first to do so. But that does not prevent the fact that we shall always be joined to one another by a silent affection, sublime to ourselves, incomprehensible to others. I am happy to know that you are well in body and strong of mind. I always predicted that your health would be good, providing that you had the courage to resist the temptations and excesses that are part of your too high-spirited character. When you find yourself surrounded by a dozen bottles of champagne, remember that tubful of water and gum arabica that I made you drain at the Hotel Danieli, and I am sure that you will have the courage to fly from them.

Good-bye, my good Alfred, love me as I love you.

Your true friend,
PIETRO PAGELLO

On the same day Alfred had written to George—(their letters took ten days to reach one another):

The man you chose can certainly not have altered your life except for the better; he's a noble creature, good and sincere; I am certain that he is devoted to you and you are too noble not to render him the same devotion. . . . But alas! I am not yet on the point of being able to interpret that terrible hieroglyphic, that word so constantly repeated —happiness! Oh my God, the whole of creation trembles with fear and hope on hearing it. Happiness! Is it the absence of desire? Is it to feel the atoms of one's being in contact with others? Is it in one's thoughts or one's senses or in one's heart—happiness? Who knows why he suffers?

. . . answer me, I implore you, that your sadness is due to your son, or to money troubles, or what do I know? to a headache, but tell me that you are happy, so that I may return to the foot of my bed, find again my resigned and brave sorrow, so that the thought of your happiness may arouse a feeble distant echo in the void in which I am, and something like a little sigh of joy in the midst of all those dreadful sobs that no one sees, if God does not exist, nor hears. . . .

George was having worries. She worried about Maurice, her nine-year-old son. She worried about her financial position, which was precarious. Pagello earned only a modest income and had no private means. However sexually rapacious George was, she was also entirely unmercenary, determined to earn her own living by journalism and literature. She finished her letter to Alfred of 26 June:

Tomorrow I am posting half of the second volume of *Jacques*. Tell and repeat again to Buloz that he will have received the whole novel by 15 July and ask him to send me the last thousands of francs by courier. I want to leave here on the 25th.

At one time she had planned to go on from Italy to Turkey. Those plans were now abandoned. After six months' absence in Venice she had remembered that she was a mother, and was apparently anxious to rejoin her children. To an old friend, Émile Paultre, she wrote on the same day:

Go and see my son and send me news of him, you would give me the greatest pleasure. . . .
I am leaving here on 25 July and shall be in Paris towards 15 August. I have good news of my daughter and Maurice informs me that she writes letters to him. God knows what letters! She does not favourize me to that extent, but I know that she prays to God every night that I may come back. Poor dear poppet. What a joy to see her again. . . .

Maurice was then nine; Solange, six.

It has too often been assumed that George Sand was a purely maternal character. This myth, invented by herself, largely to account for her failures as a lover, has been perpetuated by nearly all her biographers. But a myth it was. She dragged up her children (when she had them with her) surrounded by her Bohemian friends, making no secret in their presence of whatever liaison she might at the moment be carrying on. In 1839 she took them to Majorca with Chopin, in January, when the weather was ghastly and all four of them had to rough it in the bitterly cold and draughty monastery of Valdemosa. As she had written to Alfred, she herself, apart from occasional stomach troubles, was as strong as a horse. Maurice did not marry until late middle-age. Solange grew up extremely handsome but utterly uncontrollable, with all George's physical appetites, lazy and without a grain of talent, and passionately hating her mother.

In George's dual personality the dominant characteristic was the conflict between her strong masculinity and equally emphatic femininity. Alfred, and after him, Chopin, did not appeal to her maternal instinct as she and they were convinced, but to the protective urge which complemented her emotional dominance over them. There was nothing maternal in her relationships with her normal, lusty, male lovers, of whom she had many, such as Mérimée, Pagello, and Michel de Bourges. Her unsatisfied femininity, constantly frustrated by the male element in her personality, sought out such men in the hope of being dominated in her turn by them. But those experiments were foredoomed to failure. Virile men were either too strong-willed to be subjugated by her or too unromantic to satisfy her own sentimental ideals. As a rule she became bored with them before her unremitting demands for services of all kinds—whether emotional or practical—wore out their desires. As Marie d'Agoult wrote of her, she was greatly to be pitied.

George planned not merely to return to Paris but to make a re-entry there, even if not, at first, as triumphal as she would have liked. Alfred and others had kept her fully informed of the malicious gossip that was circulating about her. As she had written to Sainte-Beuve in 1833, she was now 'obliged' to lead her private life in public. She was undismayed at the prospect, for publicity, whether favourable or unfavourable, held no deterrents for her. And no cause ever had a more able self-advocate than George Sand's mission to vindicate George Sand.

What to do with Pagello?

They were still lovers. Alfred's glowing accounts of the young doctor to whom he had sacrificed his whole happiness naturally aroused the curiosity of Buloz and his circle regarding this medical and human paragon. If George had broken with Pietro at that moment and returned home alone her enemies might have claimed that it was he who wanted no more of her and had sent her back to France. Yet what was Pagello to do? Leave his practice, his home, all his normal contacts, to go off on such a non-professional trip? He had never been out of Italy; Paris tempted him. He was not so much interested in its glamour, history or tourist attractions, as in visiting the city's leading hospitals and watching their famous surgeons at work. He hesitated, nevertheless, to take this unusual holiday.

At last Alfred, who until then had never been able to make up his mind to write to his beloved rival, did so, most charmingly:

To my dear P. Pagello

Dear friend, it was very kind of you to write me a little note, I say little, because it was not very much. But however small the sheet of paper that tells me of your friendship, at what moment of my life would it not be gladly received? The same is perhaps not true with regard to your warnings about the wines of Champagne, and I dare not admit to the great Salvatico Pietro how well-founded was the genuine remorse I felt on reading that part of your letter. But I promise you that never, never again will I drink this accursed liquor—without deeply reproaching myself.

George tells me that you hesitate to come here with her; you must come, my friend, or not let her go. Three hundred miles are too far for a woman to travel alone. I know that she will tell you that she is as strong as a Turk. But I will whisper into your ear, very softly, that the littlest Turk is stronger than the strongest woman in Europe; believe me, who am no Turk, and come. I promise to show you, if you are interested in seeing him, one of your best friends—

Alf^d de M^t

Pagello came.

He himself seemed to know that his affair with George was drawing to a close; she was ever a bad dissembler and no doubt could barely conceal her impatience to see her 'child' again, as well as her children. Although everyone in Paris knew that Pagello was her lover, she did not take him home to her little flat on the Quai Malaquais, but arranged for him to stay in a cheap hotel, alone. The story had been spread, in order to save her face, that her Venetian lover was ennobled, a handsome young Count; and she herself introduced him to her friends as an archæologist. When they finally met this nice, simple, unpretentious and somewhat corpulent young doctor, their amazement that George could have preferred him to Alfred equalled their amusement.

From the moment the unfortunate Pietro arrived in Paris his fate was sealed. He did visit the hospitals and passed his time as best he could, for George now had very little of hers to spare for him. Possibly because he felt it incumbent upon him as a man of honour, possibly and more likely because the good-hearted fellow was genuinely hurt at her heartless treatment of him, he in his turn now began to be suspicious and jealous of Alfred. He even spoke of challenging him to a duel, though it is hard to believe that he could have meant it. The last thing George now wanted was a scene or a fight between them, which would have made her look utterly ridiculous. She took stringent precautions to prevent their meeting.

She was anxious that Alfred should not realize, or at any rate too soon, that she was no longer in love with Pagello. She swore to him that they were still happy together. She also feared the effect that seeing her again would have on him. He had to all appearances turned over a new leaf or several—those 'withered leaves', those thoughts his mind had shed. His suffering during their separation was to be read in every one of his letters; he had, he wrote over and over again, purged himself of all jealousy, wanted only her happiness. But she did not trust his vows and she had reason to dread his questioning.

Alfred had decided that he could not remain in the same city as George and Pietro. He wrote to her that his mother had given him some money—he had not a franc of his own—with which to go abroad. He would never return. He implored her to grant him one last meeting:

> You say that you are not afraid of hurting Pietro by seeing me . . . listen, listen, George, if you have a heart, let us meet anywhere, at my home or yours, at the Zoo, the cemetery, my father's tomb (where I wanted to say farewell to you . . .).
>
> . . . to know that you are unhappy, when I gave up everything to give you peace, and no farewell! ah! it's too much, too much. I am so young, my God; what have I done?

To this irresistible appeal George replied by asking him to come to her as she was ill and unable to go out; the weather was dreadful.

Their meeting passed off, no doubt with many tears, but in complete chastity. George kissed Alfred's forehead and both cheeks; that was all. He behaved throughout with tenderness and great dignity, as if he had really outgrown his boyish weakness and possessiveness at last. He seemed to believe that they would in fact never meet again. At the final moment he decided to change his plans. Instead of leaving for the Pyrenees he went to Baden in Germany to take the cure and to work on his novel:

> I shall not die until I have finished my book, on myself and you (you, especially) . . . I swear by my youth and my genius that only spotless lilies shall grow on your tomb. . . . Posterity will repeat our names like those of such immortal lovers . . . as Romeo and Juliet, Héloïse and Abélard; one will never be mentioned without the other. . . .

As soon as Alfred had left Paris George decided to return to Nohant. For formality's sake she asked her husband, who was still living there, to invite Pagello to be their guest. It is not surprising that the poor young doctor refused this formal invitation. His chief preoccupation now was how to get out of his embarrassing situation and home to Venice without dishonour. Whether or not he was genuinely jealous of Alfred at this stage, he could not very well ignore that as soon as George had returned the situation between them had once more begun to build up to its former emotional tension. Alfred, who from the moment they had met again, had with justification hoped and expected that she would come back to him (in spite of their allegedly final parting) was writing to her at Nohant, calling her his fiancée, as well as his beloved child. And George replied in a letter describing how she had given Pagello the *coup de grâce*, as usual more in sorrow than in anger:

He, who in Venice understood everything, from the moment he set foot in France has understood nothing, and he is now in despair. Everything about me hurts and irritates him, and, must I say it?, he is leaving, he has perhaps already left at this moment, and I shall not hold him back because I am offended to the depths of my souls by what he writes to me and I feel that he no longer has faith in me and therefore does not love me. If he is still in Paris I shall go there to comfort him, but not to justify myself, not to try to hold him back . . . and yet I loved him sincerely, that generous man, as romantic as myself, whom I thought stronger than myself. I loved him like a father, and you were our child. . . .

It seems that George could never love without finding some incestuous word with which to describe her feelings. There followed pages and pages of self-pity. The letter ended:

Adieu, my poor child. Ah! were it not for my own children, how gladly would I throw myself into the river!

Pagello had done everything that had been expected of him, served his purpose admirably, and George was duly

grateful. In order to obtain funds for his journey he had brought
with him some rather mediocre oil-paintings. These she sold
and with the money thus raised he was able to pay his fare
home, as well as to buy himself a case of surgical instruments
and several medical books. These seemed to have consoled
him very quickly. He returned to Venice, in due course
married and lived happily nearly 'ever afterwards' as in the
fairy-tales, for he died at the age of ninety-one, in 1898.

George may have used poor Pagello to her own ends but
he never regretted the one great affair of his life with a celebrity,
which in later years brought him several curious and some
distinguished visitors from France, to whom he would as a
special favour show the famous tea-cup out of which La Sand
had taken tea with him. But for her the aftermath of betrayal
was now to begin. However much she might have suffered
previously, it was nothing compared to the unhappiness she
was to endure in the winter of 1834.

4

Alfred returned from Germany in October.

Almost immediately they fell into each other's arms.
Whether it was because Pagello's embraces had been less
ardent than Alfred's, or whether George was now for the first
time falling in love with Alfred physically as well as romantically,
he did now, at last, awaken her senses. From loving him she
passed to being in love with him, as deeply as at any time in
her life with any man. She surrendered herself to him utterly,
body and soul. It was Alfred's moment of complete triumph.
Nothing was held back—save one thing.

It was impossible for Alfred to accept happiness in love.
He had been conditioned from childhood onwards to expect
only suffering from it and by this time he was the fated victim
of his own uncontrollable masochism. The more surely he
possessed George the more violently his own subconscious
guilt-feelings at this incestuous relationship returned to torture
him. Neither for them nor for his masochism could he find an
adequate rationalization in their present relationship. But
there remained the past, the memory of those awful weeks in

February, six months ago, when in his lucid moments between bouts of fever he had thought to catch glimpses of George and Pagello embracing one another in his sick-room. His jealousy was now entirely retrospective but none the less potent for that reason. Day after day, night after night, he plied and plagued her with questions. In between their passionate embraces the inquisition would be resumed. Had she or had she not been Pagello's mistress before he, Alfred, had accepted her pathetic confession of her love for Pietro; before he, endeavouring to rise to the noble heights of conduct demanded by his ideals, gave them his blessing, made her send for Pagello, and joined their hands together in symbolic, mystical union? What a sublime moment that had been—but how futile, how vain, how ridiculous if, at the very moment when he in his innocence had thought to make the supreme sacrifice for the sake of George's happiness she had for weeks past already been Pagello's mistress!

George was understandably in despair. She had returned to him, got rid of Pagello, given herself back to him, only to find all the old wounds reopening, bleeding; the anger, the fury, from which she had sought escape with Pagello and which Alfred had so often sworn in his letters he had completely outgrown, returned. Nevertheless, she stuck firmly to her rights and would not budge from the position she had taken up in Venice. In a long, detailed, exasperated and yet patient letter she wrote to him from Nohant—where she had once again taken refuge from the strain of their relationship—she went point by point over the whole story, carefully recapitulating it in detail. It was one of the best letters she ever wrote to him, one of the least emotional, more in sorrow than in anger, despairing and yet dignified:

Did I not foresee that you would suffer from that past that exalted you like a beautiful poem, so long as I refused to give myself back to you, and that now, when you have seized me as if I were your prey, seems like a nightmare to you? Well, let me go. We shall be more unhappy than ever. If I am as faithless and deceitful as you tell me, why do you insist on taking me back and keeping me? I did not want to love any more; I had suffered too much

If I were a coquette you would be less unhappy. I should
have lied to you, told you that I had not loved Pierre, had
never belonged to him. What prevented me from making
you believe it? It is because I was honest that you are in
tortures. Therefore one cannot love in our state and all
I did to revive our friendship was illusory! What is left
to us, my God, of a union we had thought so beautiful!
Neither love nor friendship, my God!

Put in plain, straightforward terms this plea of George's
was the essence of common sense. Their relationship was
hopeless. They were poison to one another; the only sensible
thing was to make an end. Alfred's friends entirely concurred.
They had been pressing this point of view on him for months.
Like Paul, Alfred Tattet regarded George Sand as Alfred's
evil genius. Ever since George's return they had been in a state
of uneasiness. When the lovers were reunited at the beginning
of October they watched with foreboding for the recurrence
of Alfred's nervous symptoms—insomnia, alcoholism, the
usual devil's round. Tattet had a certain influence over him,
of which George was aware. And it seemed now as if he had
temporarily won the day. Alfred left Paris for the country
and Tattet must with relief and satisfaction have read the note
he sent him before doing so:

My dear friend,
    Everything is finished. If by chance somebody [George]
asks you any questions (as it is possible that it might be
suspected that you had been talking to me) or if someone
possibly came to see you to ask if you had seen me, simply
answer no, that you have not seen me, and be sure that
our secret will be carefully guarded by me. I shall come and
see you soon.

George had in fact written to Tattet, asking him to come and
see her. For incredible as it might appear, no sooner had
she written Alfred that sensible letter, imploring him to make
an end, no sooner had he, also sensible for once, accepted the
inevitable and, to the relief of all his friends, done so, than she
set out in an absolute frenzy of desire in pursuit of him. Every

Aimée d'Alton

Rachel

string was pulled; every mutual friend was made use of. With
utter shamelessness she proclaimed to all and sundry, high and
low, her need, her misery. Her agony was discernible in her
looks, her voice, her every spoken and written word. She once
more had recourse to her 'confessor', her old friend Sainte-
Beuve.

How should one interpret this *volte-face* on George's part?
Unkindly, that she could not bear after all this time to think
that Alfred might escape her; that her hitherto unbreakable
power over him had suddenly departed? He had been, as she
had so often told him, her heart's torturer. Nevertheless, in
the past he had always suffered more from their passion than
she had. He might, now, suddenly have become a 'bird of
prey' and she its victim. But that, she must have been convinced, was merely a passing phase. Fundamentally he had
always been and still in her estimation remained her child,
the weaker, the one who would always break down first, whilst
she remained noble, strong and above all self-righteous. Now,
for the first time in their relationship, he was showing determination, obstinacy, rebelliousness, thereby upsetting its
preordained balance. This was utterly unacceptable to her
power-complex and must immediately be rectified. At all costs
the former situation must be restored. The more kindly view
suggests that only when Alfred accepted her proposal that they
should part, did she herself realize what had happened in the
previous October—that she had fallen in love with him.
At that very moment, when at last she desired him carnally,
with her body, he had escaped her. 'Desired' was too mild a
term; she needed him, longed for him, yearned for him so
passionately that his rejection of her was making her physically
ill, 'afflicted'.

It was Sainte-Beuve who used that actual term in a note he
wrote to Alfred. George had been to see him. But much as he
sympathized with her, her loyal 'confessor' advised her that
it would be better at present not to press matters further. He
wrote a note to Alfred to the same effect:

My dear friend, I came to see you to ask you no longer
to see . . . the person whom I saw this morning, so afflicted.
I was wrong to advise you to be reconciled, too soon at

any rate. Write her a kind word, but do not see her,
would hurt you both too much. Forgive my wrong advice
I hope to see you soon.

Alfred replied firmly, implacably—knowing that George
would almost certainly be shown this letter—but as usual
with dignity and charm:

> I am very grateful to you, my dear friend, for the interest
> you have taken, in these sad circumstances, in myself and
> the person of whom you tell me to-day. It is no longer
> possible for me to have any relations with her, under any
> pretext whatsoever, either in writing or otherwise. I
> hope that her friends will not see in this resolution any
> offensive intentions towards her, nor any desire to accuse
> her in any direction whatever. If anyone is to blame it is
> myself. . . . Madame Sand clearly knows my present
> intentions and if it was she who asked you to tell me no
> longer to see her, I must admit that I do not understand
> her motive, since only yesterday evening I positively
> refused to see her at my house.
>
> I repeat again, my friend, that I should be most dis
> tressed if my resolution were interpreted unfavourably as
> regards her. . . . There is *à bientôt* at the bottom of your
> card; please do not lead me to believe that it was solely
> on account of the Quai Malaquais that you remembered
> the Rue de Grenelle. You would make me appear cruel
> if you let me believe that in order to see you, I had to
> quarrel with my mistress.

He would neither see her nor communicate with her. So
instead of writing to Alfred, during that winter of 1834 George
kept a diary, her *Journal Intime*, into which she poured
all her woes. Like everything else she wrote it was destined for
ultimate publication and there is little doubt that whilst actually
writing it she visualized Alfred, one day, reading it over her
shoulder. For desperate as she was she never gave up hope
that he would in spite of his present firmness and determination
ultimately come back to her. Buloz, too, was drawn into her
confidence. He had a habit of making notes on the backs of

letters sent to him. On an invitation from George on 20 November, he scribbled:

> She admitted everything sorrowfully, throwing herself at Alfred's knees and crying: Forgive me! Bought a death's head in which to keep Alfred's last letter and more weeping at my place. . . .
> Momentary respite. alf. returns.—portrait by Delacroix. Another scene with Alfred in the evening.

He had apparently agreed to meet her in the presence of friends, although not yet alone. With Buloz she went in masculine dress to the theatre, hoping to catch a glimpse of him. She was giving sittings to the painter, Delacroix, who for all time immortalized George and her suffering in a superb portrait. This portrait would in any case have become famous, for it shows her with untidy, short, cropped hair. Yes, that was her final, desperate and magnificent gesture. She had cut off her long, shining black coils and sent them to Alfred. Could any lover, any dramatist even less obsessed than Alfred, have resisted such a gesture in the Paris of 1834? It seems improbable.

Yet it was not until 14 January 1835 that George had the incomparable satisfaction of writing the following note to Alfred Tattet:

> Sir,
> There are certain surgical operations which are very well carried out and do honour to the surgeon's skill, but which do not prevent the disease from recurring. In view of this possibility, Alfred has re-become my lover; as I assume that he will be very pleased to see you here, I invite you to dine with us on the first free day you may have. May my offences be forgotten and our friendship be restored.
> Adieu, my dear Tattet.
> > > Ever yours
> > > > George Sand.

Their reunion only lasted a bare couple of months. Was

George now, like the spider after swallowing the fly, replete? Did she admit to herself that she could never again repeat the splendid gesture of sending Alfred her locks? That therefore no such sweetly triumphant reconciliation could follow their next rupture? Or was she genuinely worn out, mentally, emotionally and physically? Whatever the reason she decided that the time had come to make an end—the end, this time. Being absolutely in earnest and not playing for effect, she set about it in her most practical vein. She had recourse to Boucoiran, Maurice's tutor, to abet her plan:

Friday, 6 March 1835

My friend,

Help me to leave today. Reserve me a seat in the coach at midday. Then come and see me. I will tell you what to do.

But if I cannot tell you, which is quite possible, for it may be very difficult for me to reassure Alfred, I will explain it to you in four words.

You will arrive here at five o'clock and with an urgent and preoccupied air you will tell me that my mother has just arrived, is very tired and rather seriously ill, that her servant is out and she needs me at once, and I must go without fail. I shall put on my hat, I shall leave, saying that I am coming back, and you will put me in the coach. Pick up my travelling bag during the day. You can easily take it away without being seen, and leave it at the Bureau. Have them arrange my travelling cushion which I am sending you. The clasp is lost.

George

Adieu, come at once if you can. But if Alf is at home do not appear to have anything to tell me. I will talk to you in the kitchen.

But she cancelled this plan in favour of a simpler one. She made a date with Alfred for the day after next and left Paris that same evening. When Alfred arrived at their love-nest on the Quai Malaquais, the bird had flown to Nohant.

Years of the phoenix

I

WHAT IS the motive power of a poet's inspiration?
In his unfinished autobiographical novel, *Le Poète Déchu*
(1839), Alfred de Musset defined it as follows:

> Have no doubts about it, the fugitive spark buried in
> a fragile brain is a divine thing. You admire a good
> instrument, a piano by Érard, a violin by Stradivarius;
> good God! and what is the human soul? Never in all the
> thirty years of my life did I develop my powers as far as I
> would have liked; I was never wholly myself except in
> silence. I have still not heard more than the first sounds
> of that melody which perhaps lies within me. This instru-
> ment will soon fall into dust; I have barely been able to tune
> it yet, with delight.
> Whomever you may be you will understand me if you
> have ever loved anything; your country, a woman, a friend,
> even less than that, your own well-being, your house, a
> room, a bed. Suppose that you are returning from a
> journey, that on entering Paris you are held up at the
> barrier by the customs. If you are capable of any emotion
> will you not feel some pleasure, some impatience, at the
> thought that soon you will again be in your house, your
> room? Does your heart not beat faster as you turn the
> corner, draw nearer and at last arrive? Well, that natural
> and commonplace pleasure, that impatience you feel to
> find again your own familiar and well-known things, let
> us suppose that you feel the same for everything that exists,
> noble or vulgar, familiar or new; suppose that your life is
> a constant journey, that every barrier is a frontier, every

inn your own house, that on every doorstep your children await you, that your wife is in every bed; you may perhaps think that I exaggerate; no, for that is how a poet feels; that is what I felt when I was twenty.

This mystical self-identification with the universe is the hall-mark of all great poets. To them it is a perpetual mystery and a perpetual revelation. They feel themselves ineluctably part of it, wedded to it in life, death and immortality. Put even more simply than Alfred put it, the source of his inspiration was love. Schiller had already immortalized it in the lines set to the last movement of his Ninth Symphony by Beethoven:

> *Seid umschlungen, Millionen,*
> *Diesen Kuss der ganzen Welt.*

The event that Alfred had so longed for, although with dread, when he was only seventeen, the great love affair that was essential to the flowering of his genius, the breaking of his inner silence into song, had come and gone. The moment had arrived to transmute his suffering into poetry.

In his biography Paul told in detail how Alfred came to write the poem that first established his claim to immortality:

One night in May his friend Alfred Tattet asked him in my presence what fruit his silence would bear, and here is his answer:

'During the past year I have re-read everything I had read previously, learned again everything I thought I already knew; I went back into society and took part in some of your amusements in order to see again what I had already seen; I made the greatest, most difficult effort to drive away the memory that still blinded me and to break the habit which would constantly recur. After having communed with my sorrow to the point at which it would no longer respond, having wept and swallowed my tears sometimes in solitude, sometimes with you, my friends who believe in me, I overcame my suffering and my past. *To-day I have with my own hands nailed down the coffin which contains my first youth, my laziness and my vanity.* I believe that at last my mind, like a plant that has been watered for a long time, has drained enough nourishment from the soil to grow up into the sunlight. It seems to me that I shall soon speak and that there is something in my soul that is striving to emerge.'

What was striving to emerge [Paul continued] was *La Nuit de Mai*. One spring evening as we were walking home, Alfred recited to me the first two verses of the dialogue between the Muse and the Poet, which he had just composed under the chestnut trees of the Tuileries. These were the lines :

LA MUSE
Poète, prends ton luth et me donne un baiser;
La fleur de l'églantier sent ses bourgeons éclore
Le printemps naît ce soir; les vents vont s'embraser,
Et la bergeronnette, en attendant l'aurore,
Aux premiers buissons verts commence à se poser.
Poète, prends ton luth et me donne un baiser.

LE POÈTE
Comme il fait noir dans la vallée!
J'ai cru qu'une forme voilée
Flottait là-bas sur la forêt.
Elle sortait de la prairie;
Son pied rasait l'herbe fleurie;
C'est une étrange rêverie;
Elle s'éfface et disparaît.

THE MUSE
Poet, take up thy lute and offer me a kiss,
The sweet-briar feels its budding petals op'ning bright,
This evening spring is born; the winds are warm with bliss.
The merry wagtail now, whilst waiting for dawn's light
On the green shoots of bushes perches not amiss.
Poet, take up thy lute and offer me a kiss.

THE POET
How dark it is down in the vale!
I thought a form wrapped in a veil
Came flitting through the forest there.
As from the meadow she did pass,
Her feet scarce brushed the flower-pied grass;
It was a vision strange and rare
That dimmed and vanished into air.

The Muse instructs the Poet in his mission, which is to love and suffer for the sake of humanity:

> Quel que soit le souci que ta jeunesse endure,
> Laisse-la s'élargir, cette sainte blessure
> Que les noirs séraphins t'ont fait au fond du coeur;
> Rien ne nous rend si grands qu'une grande douleur. . . .
> Les plus désespérés sont les chants les plus beaux,
> Et j'en sais d'immortels qui sont de purs sanglots.

> Whatever anguish thy youth may have known,
> Let it widen still deeper, that wound, Heaven's own,
> The dark seraphim tore in your suffering heart;
> Nothing makes a man greater than sorrow's sharp dart. . . .
> The most desperate songs are among the most fair,
> And the greatest of all are sobs of pure despair.

The Muse then compares the poet with the pelican, the bird who, to feed his hungry young, plucks the flesh from his own breast, a mystical concept derived from early Christian symbolism and now developed in long, superb lines that ring like the pounding of waves on some desolate and distant shore:

> Lui, gagnant à pas lents une roche élevée,
> De son aile pendante abritant sa couvée,
> Pêcheur mélancholique, il regarde les cieux.
> Le sang coule à longs flots de sa poitrine ouverte,
> En vain il a des mers fouillé la profondeur:
> L'Océan était vide et la plage déserte;
> Pour toute nourriture il apporte son coeur. . . .
> Mais parfois, au milieu du divin sacrifice,
> Fatigué de mourir dans un trop long supplice,
> Il craint que ses enfants ne le laissent vivant,
> Alors il se soulève, ouvre son aile au vent,
> Et se frappant le coeur avec un cri sauvage,
> Il pousse dans la nuit un si funèbre adieu
> Que les oiseaux des mers désertent le rivage,
> Et que le voyageur attardé sur la plage,
> Sentant passer la mort, se recommende à Dieu.
> Poète, c'est ainsi que font les grand poètes. . . .
> Leurs déclamations sont comme des épées;
> Elles tracent dans l'air un cercle éblouissant,
> Mail il y pend toujours quelque goutte de sang.

Sadly the poet replies:

> J'ai vu le temps où ma jeunesse
> Sur mes lèvres était sans cesse
> Prête à chanter comme un oiseau;
> Mais j'ai souffert un dur martyre,
> Et le moins que j'en pourrais dire,
> Si je l'essayais sur ma lyre,
> La briserait comme un roseau.

Then to a rocky eminence he slowly paces,
And as his progeny his wing embraces,
He scans the heavens with a desperate eye.
Blood spurts in torrents from his bosom's wound.
In vain the depths of ocean did he sound,
The beach was bare, wherever he did dart,
He brought home nothing save his breaking heart.
But sometimes, in this sacrifice sublime,
He fears his death will drag too long a time
And that his children will not let him die.
So then he rises, spreading wings to wind,
And beats his breast with such a savage cry
That all the sea-birds fly from off the sod,
And the lone traveller on the shore nearby
Hearing death pass, commends himself to God.
That, poet, is what all great poets do. . . .
Their verse as keen as rapier on their lip
Traces a brilliant circle in the sky,
But always with some blood-drop at its tip.

THE POET

There was a time when youth would sing
On my lips, forever carolling
As merry as a bird, indeed,
But I have suffered hard and long
And if today I sang a song
And on my lyre it were to ring
'Twould break it like a reed.

Paul's story continued:

He worked without stopping until dawn. When he
came in to breakfast I saw no signs of fatigue on his features.
. . . The Muse possessed him. During the day he went on

talking and working turn and turn about, like those chess-players who play two games at a time. He would leave us to go and write ten lines of verse, then return and continue talking. But in the evening he went back to work as if he were keeping a love-tryst. He had a light supper served in his room. He would gladly have had two places laid so that the Muse should find hers prepared for her. All the lights were pressed into service; he lit a dozen candles. Seeing these illuminations the other people in the house might have thought that he was giving a ball. At dawn on the second day, the poem being finished, the Muse flew away, but she had been so lovingly entertained that she promised to return. The poet blew out his candles, went to bed and slept until the following evening. When he awoke he read through his verses, but found that they needed no re-touching.

2

The physical and emotional strain of the creative process was followed by a period of exhaustion. The Muse was a mistress no less demanding than any flesh-and-blood woman. Alfred suffered in the course of coming down to earth from the heights to which she had led him. The chief symptom of this reaction was a sense of profound melancholy and ennui. In his efforts to shake off this depression

It appeared [wrote Paul] that all the luxury of Sardan-opolis, the most varied and subtle distractions Paris could offer, hardly sufficed. . . .

Yet Paul indignantly and with a convincing argument refuted the allegations of Alfred's alleged excesses at this time:

In order to expose the stupidity and malevolence of such tittle-tattle . . . it is only necessary to list here the works he produced in the course of the year 1835; these were: *Lucie, La Nuit de Mai, La Quenouille de Barbarine, Le Chandelier, La Loi sur la Presse, La Nuit de Décembre* and *La Confession d'un Enfant du Siècle*. When would he have found time to write so much had he been spending his nights dining and wining and his days in sleeping off his nocturnal dissipations?

One of the most remarkable points about the works produced by Alfred during this phoenix year of his life is their diversity and variety, both in form and content.

Lucie was a minor poem, *La Nuit de Mai*, a masterpiece. *La Quenouille de Barbarine* was a slight three-act prose comedy. *Le Chandelier*, almost equally short, was also a prose play. But here, as in *Les Caprices de Marianne*, Alfred was only half flippant and more than half autobiographical.

Fortunio, the hero of *Le Chandelier*, is a very young and still innocent Alfred, a clerk articled to an elderly lawyer, whose young wife is having an affair with Clavaroche, an officer. At his suggestion Jacqueline, in order to divert her husband's suspicions, flirts with Fortunio and pretends to be in love with him, as he is with her. When he discovers her stratagem Fortunio expresses his bitter disillusionment in a monologue:

'. . . to lie with all one's heart, to use one's body as bait, to make game of what is most sacred under heaven, like a thief with loaded dice; that is what makes a woman smile!'

yet *Le Chandelier* is a comedy and in the end Fortunio wins a repentant Jacqueline from Clavaroche. It sparkles with witty lines:

'When one cannot prove that one is in the right, one is in the wrong . . . A jealous husband's suspicions cannot roam the void; they are not swallows. They must settle somewhere sooner or later and the safest thing is to prepare a nest for them.

'All soldiers look alike; whoever loves one, loves a hundred.'

The next poem that Alfred wrote after *La Nuit de Mai* was not another love poem. It had the prosaic title, *La Loi sur la Presse*.

Alfred de Musset was accused by his detractors of many faults, among them acute self-absorption and almost complete indifference to public affairs. This was by no means true. He was very much aware of his historical background and social environment and of the politics of his time. He was by birth and personal predilection an aristocrat. Léon Séché told the following amusing story about him:

> One evening when a little friend of his, a dancer at the Opera, was dining with a certain prince, Musset arrived in time for dessert, sat down, and offered the ballerina a peach, telling her some light-hearted tale about the good effects on young ladies of peaches. Somewhat embarrassed, she asked him if he thought she was a Joan of Arc? He then raised his eyebrows and replied in a very different tone: 'I would like you to know that Joan of Arc was my great-grand aunt.'

And he was not joking, for the Mussets were by marriage connected with the Maid of Orleans's family. He had been a brilliant scholar and had an excellent analytical brain. Temperamentally he found the heavier professions such as the law or the civil service uncongenial. But almost from his boyhood onwards he had regarded himself as a professional man of letters. Liberty of thought, speech and publication was as precious to him as to any of his colleagues.

On 28 July 1835 a revolutionary called Fieschi made an attempt on the life of the king, Louis-Philippe. His Prime Minister, Thiers, seized this opportunity to bring in a repressive law, 'la loi sur la presse', containing severe penalties for so-called incitement of the population, or evil intent. Alfred de Musset promptly wrote a long satirical poem of thirty-four stanzas addressed to Thiers, which he published in the following month. In this he vigorously upheld the cause of literary freedom in passionately rhetorical lines:

> Une loi sur la presse! ô peuple gôbe-mouche!
> La loi, pas vrai? quel mot! comme il emplit la bouche!
> Une loi maternelle et qui vous tend les bras!
> Une loi, notez-bien, qui ne *réprime* pas
> Qui supprime! Une loi comme *sainte-nitouche*,
> Une petite loi, qui marche à petits pas!

This image of a maternal law, holding out its arms to the simple-minded citizens with intent not to reprimand but to suffocate and suppress, still has validity; for in our time also dictatorships invariably begin by nibbling away at the people's freedom 'for their own good'.

It was not for nothing that Alfred de Musset entitled his one long novel (which he was then writing) *The Confession of a Child of this Century*. For he was acutely conscious of his period and he loathed and despised the world into which he had been born. It seemed to him utterly lacking in the heroic virtues, uninspired and uninspiring, vulgar and sordid.

There is no doubt that throughout his life Alfred felt the lack of some great incentive, of some noble cause to which he might have devoted and even sacrificed himself. He was a Byron without a Greece, a Prince of Denmark without a kingdom. Whether rightly or wrongly, he despised most of his contemporaries as much as himself. It was this sense of futility, which he described with such moving despair in the *Confession*, that weighed upon him all his life and coupled with his guilt-feelings in regard to sex, drove him to dissipation. He had already been aware of it at seventeen, when he had written those macabre letters to his school-fellow, Paul Foucher. As he grew older his ennui increased and his frantic efforts to disperse it dragged him deeper and deeper into debauchery. He claimed to have written his *Confession* as a warning to young men of his day and when it was published they responded to it.

2

The Muse had promised to return.

One evening [wrote Paul] as I was coming home towards midnight, in frightful weather, I saw so many lights in my brother's room that I thought he must be entertaining several friends. He was writing *La Nuit de Décembre*.

Paul went out of his way to record that this, the second of the four great *Nuits*, was inspired by an altogether different person, a society woman with whom Alfred at the beginning of 1835 apparently had an affair that lasted three weeks. If it did refer to such a person Alfred must have taken this short episode extremely tragically, even for him. But there is no doubt at all that once again (as he was to do on three more occasions before his heartbreak's poetic inspiration was spent) he was immortalizing his passion for George in these great verses.

La Nuit de Décembre was not written in dialogue form. It is the famous poem in which he describes and interrogates his *alter ego*, his double, 'as like me as a looking-glass' who at the end reveals that his name is Loneliness. Although in the *Confession* Alfred had taken all the blame for his rupture with George on himself, the cathartic effect of writing the novel was by no means complete:

> Partez, partez, la Nature immortelle
>   N'a pas tout voulu vous donner.
> Ah! pauvre enfant, qui voulez être belle,
>   Et ne savez pas pardonner!
> Allez, allez, suivez la destinée!
>   Qui vous perd n'a pas tout perdu.
> Jetez au vent notre amour consumé—
>   Éternel Dieu! toi que j'ai tant aimé,
>   Si tu pars, pourquoi m'aimes-tu?
>
> Depart, depart, immortal Nature
>   To you not all would give.
> Poor child, who wanted to be fair of feature,
>   But learned not to forgive!
> Then go, then go, fulfilling your own fate!
>   Not all is lost by him who has lost you.
> Throw to the winds our love, so dear of late—
>   Eternal God! so deeply I loved you,
>   But if you go, why did you love me, too?

The woman described in this poem, madly proud, deceitful, a liar, who 'learned not to forgive', she from whom Nature had withheld the final gift—the capacity at the supreme moment to give herself—who but George could successfully read between those accusing lines and recognize herself?

The series of great poems that had begun in May 1835

continued during the following year. In February 1836, during the height of the carnival season, Alfred had tried to distract himself by taking part in the orgiastic festivities that were customary at that period. But such distraction brought him no inner peace and was succeeded by profound melancholy. Once again he shut himself into his room, brooding on the carnival of the previous year, shortly before his final parting from George, re-living those heart-breaking weeks. To appease his agony he turned to his books and re-read the *Méditations* of his contemporary, Lamartine.

Alphonse de Lamartine was Alfred's senior by twenty years, an established poet who, although a Romantic, was strongly influenced by the classical tradition and also devoutly Catholic. A liberal politically, he was a member of the Chamber of Deputies and became head of the provisional government during the Revolution of 1848. He possessed many qualities that Musset lacked, particularly political ambition and will-power.

Now, in his despair, Alfred had sought consolation in the elder poet's verse. In the *Lettre à Lamartine* he expressed his admiration and gratitude. It opens with a long reference to Byron and his love of Greece, an inspiration to them both. The middle part contains a dramatic and powerful description of the sordid orgies of the carnival, in the midst of which the author re-lives his suffering. At the end he affirms his belief in God and his hope one day to find peace with God's help.

In the meantime, to cure himself of this love which had so nearly destroyed him, Alfred was determined to love again. 'Not all is lost by him who has lost you', he had written to George in *La Nuit de Décembre*. Six months later, in June 1836, the Muse looked in, but her place was not prepared and she withdrew. More prosaically, Alfred had begun to write a *Nuit de Juin* when his friend Tattet called to take him to a party. One night in August, however, the candles were lit again and the Muse was joyously welcomed. The dialogue opens with her gentle chiding of the negligent poet. But the tone of this poem is one of triumph; conscious of his youth and virility, the poet ends with a paean in praise of love, of which the lyrical sweep and exuberance have never been surpassed:

O Muse, que m'importe ou la mort ou la vie?
J'aime et je veux pâlir; j'aime et je veux souffrir;
J'aime, et pour un baiser je donne mon génie;
J'aime et je veux sentir sur ma lèvre amaigrie
Ruisseler une source impossible à tarir,
J'aime et je veux chanter la joie et la paresse,
Ma folle expérience et mes soucis d'un jour,
Et je veux raconter et répéter sans cesse
Qu'après avoir juré de vivre sans maîtresse,
J'ai fait serment de vivre et de mourir d'amour.

Dépouilles devant tous l'orgueil qui te dévore,
Coeur gonflé d'amertume et qui t'es cru fermé.
Aimes, et tu renaîtras; fais-toi fleur pour éclore.
Après avoir souffert, il faut souffrir encore;
Il faut aimer sans cesse, après avoir aimé.

O Muse, do I care if I die or I live?
I love, would grow pale and would suffer for love,
I love, for a kiss all my genius I'd give,
I love, on my dry lips once more I would feel
Inexhaustible springs in their onrushing flow.
I love, and would sing of my laze and my pleasure,
I will tell and repeat that the whole world shall know
Of my crazy experience, the fruits of my leisure.
Having sworn for no mistress in future to live,
I now swear that for love to my death I will go.

Reveal to the full your devouring pride,
O heart I thought bitter, and e'er to love closed,
Love again, and revive, like the new budding rose,
Having suffered, now suffer again and again,
He must love without end, who has once known love's pain.

Love is still equated with suffering, but that no longer
matters, for it is the sole source of inspiration and only through
this self-immolation to the demands of love can the poet's
heart re-open like a flower.

Yet even the delights and comparatively small sorrows of a
new love had not banished George from Alfred's memory.
The recollection of that moment when he had thought himself
to be making the most 'sublime' gesture of his life, when he had
formally renounced her to Pagello, to discover later that they

Rachel as *Phèdre*

Cartoons by Alfred de Musset, from his sketch-book illustrating the courtship of Pauline Garcia by Henri Viardot:

(Collection of M. Olivier de Grandcourt de Musset)

were already lovers, rankled like a poisoned dart. Only the Muse could help him to transmute hatred and bitterness (for that was what he now felt when he remembered his shameful betrayal by George) into love and forgiveness.

On a wild October night in 1836 the candles were lit again, the curtains drawn, and *La Nuit d'Octobre* was born. At the Muse's request the poet tells her of his anguish in short, sharp lines, like cries of despair and malediction:

> Honte à toi qui la première
> M'as appris la trahison,
> Et d'horreur et de colère
> M'as fait perdre la raison.
> Honte à toi, femme à l'oeil sombre
> Dont les funestes amours
> Ont enseveli dans l'ombre
> Mon printemps et mes beaux jours!
>
> Honte à toi! tu fus la mère
> De mes premières douleurs,
> Et tu fis de ma paupière,
> Jaillir la source des pleurs!
> Elle coule, sois-en sûre,
> Et rien ne la tarira;
> Elle sort d'une blessure
> Qui jamais ne guérira;
> Mais dans cette source amère
> Du moins je me laverai,
> Et j'y laisserai, j'espère,
> Ton souvenir abhorré!
>
> Shame on thee, who first of all,
> Taught me to know treason,
> By whom in rage and horror's thrall
> I was deprived of reason.
> Shame on thee and those dark eyes
> That poisoned love's delight,
> And buried in the shade of lies
> My springtime fair and bright.
>
> Shame on thee, the mother, thou,
> Of my first pain, that sears
> And from my eyelids caused to flow
> The fountain of my tears.

I

It flows, of that be ever sure,
Nor ever will be sealed.
From deep within, a wound impure,
Not to be stilled nor healed.
Yet in this well of bitterness
I shall my sorrow stay,
And wash away without regress
Thy hated memory!

At this point the Muse kindly but firmly interrupts the
poet:

Poète, c'est assez . . .

and in long caressing lines reproves him for his bitterness,
reminding him that the faithless beauty should not be hated
but pitied, for although it was her destiny to break his heart,
she too suffered:

Dans ses larmes, crois-moi, tout n'était pas mensonge.
Quand tout l'aurait été, plains-la! Tu sais aimer.

The Muse's consoling phrases are so gently maternal that
their magic almost makes one overlook the fact, when reading
them, that they were written by the poet himself. He gratefully
accepts her advice and although the poem now reverts to the
previous dramatic short stanza, it ends with a noble vow: to
forget, forgive, and live for the happiness a sweeter love has
brought him.

Once more, many years later, Alfred was to recall that bitter
love, but still forgivingly, in the last of his great poems inspired
by George, entitled *Souvenir*.

⤗⤗⤗ VIII ⤙⤙⤙

The Muse in lighter vein

I

EVER SINCE Alfred's return from Venice, Paul and Tattet had been urging him to take up his social life again. His rich and dandified young friends were only too pleased to welcome him back. The publication of his poems and plays in the *Revue des deux Mondes* had aroused their admiration and respect. They and even more their ladies were prepared to make a small cult of this handsome, heart-broken young poet, who, although he wrote such charming verse and prose, remained a gentleman.

Lamartine received the poem dedicated to him—and its author—affably enough. But in spite of Alfred's increasing evidence of genius, at least as great as if not surpassing their own, neither he nor any of the other more serious men of literature would accept him as an equal. To them he remained a dilettante, a playboy, and his plays remained buried for ten years in the *Revue*.

The *Revue des deux Mondes* provided Alfred with only a meagre income, but at least published everything he wrote. In the spring of 1835 Buloz invited him to write a review of the paintings exhibited in the *Salon*. Although Alfred himself had long ceased to be a painter, his interest in art, both classical and contemporary, remained throughout his life.

It was a lovely spring and summer. One morning in April he was correcting the proofs of the *Salon* article by his open window. Glancing across the courtyard, he saw at a window opposite a very pretty girl. They exchanged smiles; very soon this flirtation at a distance became a closer one. They met in the street, a rendezvous was arranged, and in a short time an idyll had developed between them.

The girl's name was Louise. She was not a lady but a working-girl, who earned her living as a seamstress. She belonged

129

to that class of girls who, although they worked long hours at
at a highly skilled trade for pathetically small wages, were
always gay, high-spirited, charming, with that carefree charm
typical of the girls of Paris. Although their moral code was
relatively elastic, if they took a lover it was for no ulterior,
mercenary motive and when they lost their hearts they did not
lose their common sense or their self-respect. Such attractive
young women were known in Alfred's time as *grisettes* because
they or some of them in earlier times had worn cheap and
simple little dresses of grey cotton that they themselves made.
This was no longer the case at the beginning of the nineteenth
century, when they blossomed out in gayer colours. But the
name and its charm still clung to them. (Their present-day
successors have become known as *midinettes*, and at midday,
in the fashionable quarters of Paris, can still be seen tumbling
out of the workshops or ateliers of the dressmakers for their
luncheon break like a flock of bright, chattering little birds.)
The term was already used at a much earlier period. In *La
Joconde*, La Fontaine wrote:

> Sous les cotillons des grisettes
> Peut loger autant de beauté
> Que sous les jupes des coquettes,

a gallantly French precedent of Kipling's

> For the Colonel's lady an' Judy O'Grady
> Are sisters under their skins.

Louise was soon head over heels in love with her handsome
young poet. Alfred had been invited by his friend Tattet to
spend some weeks at that rich young man's country house.
When he left Paris, Louise was inconsolable, and wrote him
some simple but touching letters. Tattet had a little cottage
tucked away in the woods on his father's estate, which he
offered to Alfred, who returned to town, picked up Louise
and bore her off there. There was nothing sinister or macabre
about their nightly excursions and promenades in those woods
by moonlight; no horrid phantoms appeared either to Alfred
or his companion to mar their simple bliss. In the sunshine
and the country air, among the trees and the flowers, Louise

gave rein to her instinctive gaiety. In due course they returned to Paris where they gradually drifted apart, with no scenes or recriminations, although no doubt with a few tears.

It is to Louise that we owe the delightful story of *Frédéric et Bernerette* which Alfred published a couple of years later and either to her or one of her successors his even more famous *Mimi Pinson*, sub-titled *Profil de grisette*, a little masterpiece containing the famous song of Mimi Pinson herself:

> Mimi Pinson est une blonde,
> Une blonde que l'on connaît.
> Elle n'a qu'une robe au monde
>   Landerinette!
> Et qu'un bonnet.

> Mimi Pinson porte une rose,
> Une rose blanche au côté,
> Cette fleur dans son coeur éclose,
>   Landerinette!
>   C'est la gaieté.

> Mimi Pinson is a blonde,
>   A blonde to all well-known,
> She has but one dress in the world,
>   Landerinette
> And one bonnet to call her own.

> Mimi Pinson wears a rose,
>   At her waist a white rose is seen,
> A flower, too, in her heart grows,
>   Landerinette
>   'Tis gaiety I mean.

At the supper-party at which she sang this famous song Mimi also entertained her admirers with the local gossip of the quarter, St. Germain-des-Prés:

> . . . The son of one of the richest bankers in Paris had offered a celebrated seamstress a box at the Opera and a country house, which she had refused, preferring to take care of her parents and to remain faithful to a shop-walker at the Deux-Magots. . . .

In those days the Deux-Magots on the corner of the Rue
de Seine was a well-known draper's shop, outside which hung
a sign portraying the two Chinese sages from which it took its
name, and which, wrote Balzac (quoted by Maurice Allem
in his edition of Alfred de Musset's works) 'was one of the busiest
shops in the capital, with up to thirty employees'.

Never was more enchanting tribute paid to the working
girls of Paris than *Mimi Pinson*.

In between the joyous *Nuit d'Aout* and the tragic *Nuit
d'Octobre*, Alfred wrote a poem that was also a tribute, but to
a very different kind of person indeed.

On 23 September 1836, Parisian music-lovers were plunged
into mourning by news of the death in Manchester of Marie
Malibran, one of the most beautiful women of the period, and
one of the greatest opera singers of all time. She was twenty-
eight. She was the star of the Italian Opera and when only
seventeen had made a sensational success at Covent Garden, in
Rossini's *Barber of Seville*. Alfred was among her most fervent
admirers, and may have heard Malibran sing in the salon of the
Comtesse Marie d'Agoult, where she appeared several times,
accompanied at the piano by Rossini himself, who doted on her.
When Alfred heard of her death he wrote a very long and
moving poem of twenty-seven verses, which ended with the
lines:

> Meurs donc! ta mort est douce et ta tâche est remplie.
> Ce que l'homme ici-bas appelle le génie,
> C'est le besoin d'aimer; hors de là tout est vain.
> Et puisque tôt ou tard l'amour humain s'oublie,
> Il est d'une grande âme et d'un heureux destin
> D'expirer comme toi pour un amour divin!

He had barely met her when he paid this funereal tribute
to the great singer but nevertheless, wrote Paul,

> One day in a railway carriage I heard some strangers
> talking about my brother, regretting that Madame
> Malibran had not responded to his love for her, which
> might have saved that young and charming poet from
> another, more dangerous love. . . . There was, however, a

slight difficulty: for only once in his life did Alfred de Musset see Madame Malibran elsewhere than on the stage, in a salon where she was singing, and he had not even spoken to her.

Later on, however, he was to become more deeply involved emotionally with her sister, Pauline Garcia, who was also a great artist.

2

Among Alfred's rich and aristocratic friends was a lady, Madame Caroline Jaubert. She was tiny as a fairy; her slippers were so small that her admirers collected them and placed them among the little ornaments on their *étagères*. She had no special claims to beauty, but made up for her lack of looks and inches by the gift of indescribable charm. She had a subtle mind, was an acute observer of the social scene, witty, and the centre of a brilliant circle of which Alfred was the favourite. One evening when they were all playing a game of 'Nicknames' Caroline baptised him *Le Prince Café*, because he was so stimulating and for his glittering and inconstant quality, *Le Prince Phosphore-de-Coeur-Volant*. He, in return, called her his *Marraine*—godmother—and himself her *fieux*, the older version of *filleul*, or godson.

He was never in love with her, yet he loved her more genuinely than any other woman save George. For Caroline was a true mother-surrogate to him, a fairy godmother indeed. If anyone ever understood him, she did; she became his 'confessor', somewhat as Sainte-Beuve became George's. In her he found a *confidante* to whom he could explain himself and his problems simply, sincerely, without posing, without a trace of play-acting or exaggerated emotion.

All his life Alfred was plagued by the mystery of his own personality. He dramatized it in his plays and poems, although he could not thus explain it to himself. But he described it to Caroline Jaubert. She had the courage never to flatter or spoil him and in her desire to help him, dared to tell him frankly the uncomplimentary things that had been said about him.

Like many hypersensitive people Alfred was easily embarrassed, even shy, and to hide his embarrassment—especially as he grew older or when he was unsober—often protected himself by assuming a gruff or sometimes downright rude manner. He could acept Caroline's reproofs:

> I thank you for having told me the things that have been said about me . . . I particularly like your gentle, kind and yet sincere manner of reproaching and even condemning without hurting one, you have that most precious of gifts; it is natural to you. . . .
> . . . I detest myself in such moments. They are not me. That is not my nature. When I was a child I was quite different. You tell me that I drive away men of intelligence and good feeling who are drawn towards me. Yes, it is true, and do you think that I do not know it? and that I do not sometimes regret it? I have looked at myself and asked myself whether under that stiff, grumpy, impertinent and unsympathetic exterior there was not something primitive and passionate, exalted, as in the case of Rousseau.

She had tried to find a name for the affection they felt for one another, but had not succeeded in doing so:

> You have found [Alfred wrote to her] the right name for the feeling which unites us when you call it a feeling that has no name. . . .

In her presence, he added, his heart which in the company of so many other people 'contracted', was able to expand.

It might have been a difficult relationship for Madame Jaubert to sustain for so many years if she was in love with him. Although Alfred's affection for her was deep its limits were clearly defined. But she was a woman of the world to her small finger-tips and seems to have had no trouble at all in balancing for so long on this emotional tight-rope. Like most of his friends or lovers Caroline served him for a model. In the person of Madame de Léry, the fascinating heroine of his playlet, *Un Caprice*, he drew a most endearing portrait of her.

3

He was now getting on for thirty but still living at home in his mother's flat in the Rue de Grenelle, with her, Paul and their much younger sister Hermine. Although his family were his most loyal admirers, they were perturbed by the fact that he had no fixed position in life and earned nothing except trifling sums from the publication of his works in the *Revue des deux Mondes*. Alfred had for years been living above his own means and showed no signs of settling down.

In 1846, the family decided to sell a small estate which had come down to them. Alfred's share of the first instalment of the payment arrived one morning—five thousand francs in cash, the largest sum he had ever received. Paul prudently advised him to invest it. 'What?' exclaimed Alfred, 'change good solid *écus* into scraps of paper? Not on my life. I shall not entrust this money to the State, but to my wardrobe.' As a precaution against spending it too quickly, however, he locked it up and gave the key to Paul, saying that he was never to give him any of the money in the evening, when he might gamble it away. Paul took it and went into the salon with a caller, General de Berthois. As soon as they had sat down for a chat, Alfred followed, bent down and whispered to him: 'Give me the key.' Paul did so and never saw it again. The five thousand francs soon vanished into the kitties of the gambling dens of Paris.

From time to time discussions took place as to various posts he might occupy, but nothing ever came of them. His former school-friend, now the Duke of Orleans, had not forgotten their boyhood friendship. After another attempt on the King's life—the fourth—in 1836, Alfred wrote a sonnet expressing his thankfulness at his escape. Tattet saw that a copy reached the Duke, who wrote the poet a very friendly note on New Year's Day, 1837. When Alfred called to pay his respects the Duke had the sonnet in his pocket and went in to show it to His Majesty in person. He emerged from the Royal presence with some embarrassment. The King had not appreciated this tribute because in it he had been addressed with poetic licence, in the second person singular! So the Royal heir did not present the poet to his monarch until a later occasion.

'Ah!' said Louis-Philippe with a most affable smile, 'so you have come from Joinville; I am very pleased to see you.'

Alfred made no reply but merely bowed deeply. The King had in fact mistaken him for a cousin who was a forestry inspector on the Royal estates.

After the Duke of Orleans's marriage a minor post, that of librarian at the Ministry of the Interior, became vacant and the Prince used his influence to help his former school-fellow to obtain it. The duties involved were not heavy and never seemed to have interfered either with Alfred's literary work or or with his social activities.

4

Many a time his mother and his old friend the Duchesse de Castries must have decided that all Alfred needed to steady him—to put an end to his gambling, his fondness for wild parties, his tendency to inebriation—was some 'nice girl' with a reasonable dowry who would make him a suitable wife. Caroline Jaubert, like so many respectable society women, adored amorous intrigues of all kinds. When at her house Alfred met Aimée d'Alton, a cousin of hers, his fond Mama may well have had hopes that a suitable candidate had at last appeared who would cure him of his wildness, help him to forget the suffering of his love for George Sand and enable him at last successfully to settle down.

Aimée d'Alton was only a year younger than Alfred, a very pretty girl, with golden hair, blue eyes and a lovely fair complexion. She was well educated, intelligent and self-possessed. When she met Musset she immediately fell in love with him. She had, of course, read his verses, plays and the *Confession*; she knew his reputation for fast living and gambling, which probably increased his fascination for her. Few young girls in love with a rake can resist the challenge to reform him. Aimée set about it subtly, in a manner calculated to amuse and intrigue him. The little home-made pills were dipped in the sweetest of jam. He had admitted to her that he was lazy; she sent him a pen-holder in a sandalwood box, as an inducement to write. He had confessed that he also gambled,

o she made him a little silk purse, such as men-about-town
carried in their waistcoat pockets, put a gold piece into it
and sent it to him anonymously with a note which said:
Do not spend too quickly what I contain; when you go out,
put just one gold piece in me; that is enough for one day'.
This was the basis of the plot of *Un Caprice*, although
Aimée was not the heroine of this playlet.

These were not the first tokens of gallantry Alfred had
received from women, but the implied flattery of such gifts
never failed to arouse his interest. Aimée had a fairly serious
illness and went away to the country to recuperate from it.

> . . . My hand trembles as I write to you . . . but receive
> this letter as I received yours, perhaps with some surprise,
> but tell yourself that it comes from a heart that truly beats
> for you. . . . When are you coming back? Shall I still be
> here?

The Duke of Orleans had offered Alfred a diplomatic post
in Madrid, but he did not accept it. It was assumed that this
was because of his love for Aimée. It is more probable that this
new affair gave him an excuse to himself for refusing the
Spanish assignment. Apart from his librarianship, which was
practically a sinecure, Alfred avoided any permanent employ-
ment with enthusiasm. All that was necessary to confirm his
refusal was Aimée's advice that he should accept. He was now
convinced that he was in love with her. She wrote that she
had been ill, was still not strong and had to spend a lot of time
resting on a chaise-longue. Wittily Alfred rejoined:

> You say that your health is an invincible obstacle; I
> do not recognize any such impediment to love, and a
> chaise-longue is not such an ugly piece of furniture that
> one need speak ill of it.

She still held back, fearing that they might not be happy.
To this anxiety Alfred had a typically Musset answer:

> I am only a year older than you, but ten years older in
> experience. Do not smile at that word . . . let me tell you

what my experience has taught me. It is the first, inevitable
longing of a loving heart to dream fine dreams and to
attempt to realize them. . . . But, Aimée, one's first experience is to learn to suffer; to discover that no dream ever
comes *completely* true, or that if they do, they wither and
die when they come into contact with reality. Nevertheless,
one goes on living and one has to go on loving in order to
live. One loves although one is afraid to do so, defiantly,
but gradually on looking around, one discovers that life is
not as sad as one had thought; one returns to happiness,
to God, to truth. A heart that has become resigned is more
grateful for its happy days; longs for them more ardently
and is more careful to prolong them. And finally, one can
say that pain is nothing, since happiness exists. That is
my experience, Aimée, that I would like to share with you,
if I had any power over your kind and noble heart. It is
not the conclusion of the book you like, and which is no
less true for that reason, but it is the sequel to it, whatever must be the result. . . .

The book in question was his *Confession*. There can be
no doubt that when he wrote this touching letter to Aimée,
Alfred believed quite sincerely what he told her—that this
new, pure, tender love he felt for her would be, must be, his
salvation; would lead him back to God and happiness. It
was hardly likely that Aimée would resist such a candid and
tender appeal. She wrote that she would come back to Paris in
May. Alfred was in transports of joy:

Ah! how right you are to return with the flowers, the
foliage, and the sun! Call me mad, if you like . . . but I feel
that with your first kiss a flower will blossom in my heart.
And yet you dare speak of sadness! You dare be anxious.
God does not lie, my white rose, and he would lie if we
were not to be happy! . . . dear, dear Aimée, how happy
I am to be alive and to have known you.

Aimée overcame her scruples and in that lovely summer of
1837 gave herself to Alfred. She was madly in love with him.
Certainly she was convinced of her mission to reform him.

And maybe like other courageous girls in a similar situation she hoped that by this gift of her body she might in due course become his wife. She certainly had courage. Where were they to meet? Alfred had no money and still lived at home. Would she come to him there? As he wrote the letter in which he asked her to do so, as she read it, necessity was clothed in a delightful aura of romance and intrigue:

> Our apartment is not very large and there are my mother, my brother, my sister, and three servants . . . are you afraid, lovely cherub? Let me tell you that this whole houseful of people lies snoring on its ears, invariably, until half-past eight or nine o'clock, masters and servants all. Not a soul is about. So in asking you to come between 7 and 8, I am being excessively careful. . . .

Aimée came. Alfred awaited her in his flowered dressing-gown, his nose glued to the window-pane, ran downstairs to let her in and together they tiptoed back, through the dining-room, which they had to cross to reach his room. If Madame de Musset did happen to awake she may well have closed her eyes again with a thankful sigh.

During the next few months, Aimée's influence on Alfred was admirable. He decided that they must find a love-nest of their own and set to work seriously to earn the money to pay for it. He wrote *Un Caprice*, and when it was published in the *Revue*, Aimée was enchanted. Aimée became the heroine of a short story, *Le Fils du Titien*, in which Alfred drew her portrait as the beautiful Beatrix Donato, who is also determined to reform her lover, Pippo. She succeeds so well that he paints her portrait as 'Venus in Love'. But the story ends with a slightly sinister twist. All night long Beatrix remained awake, excited by her triumph, seeing her lover praised by all Italians, bestowing through his incomparable art, to which she had led him back, glory on himself and his native city of Venice. When next morning, however, Beatrix went to meet Pippo, and whilst waiting for him examined the portrait again, she saw that on a rock in the foreground of the picture he had written a sonnet in fine Gothic characters. In this he proclaimed her beauty, his love for her, and his determination, because this was his

masterpiece, never during the rest of his life to paint another
picture. The story ends:

> In spite of all her efforts, Beatrix was never able to
> induce her lover to work again; all her prayers left him
> inflexible, and when she pressed him too hard, he recited
> his sonnet to her. He thus remained faithful unto death to
> his laziness; and Beatrix, so they tell, to their love. . . .

No other writer ever surpassed Alfred's talent for speaking
true words in jest, for wrapping up unpleasant and even cruel
home-truths in delightful verse or prose.

In August they were still happy. Alfred wanted to love
Aimée, he tried with all his heart to do so. She was the perfect
antidote for his past pain. She was beautiful, kind, intelligent,
understanding—flawless, in fact. But she could not and never
did cause him a moment's suffering. The first signs of restlessness appeared towards the end of September, when Alfred
wrote to her that he had felt a sudden mood of appalling
anguish. And in the following month *La Nuit d'Octobre* revealed
the struggle that was going on in his heart. It ended on a
hopeful note:

> N'as tu pas maintenant une belle maîtresse?
> Et lorsqu'en t'endormant tu lui serre la main,
> Le lointain souvenir des maux de ta jeunesse
> Ne rend-il pas plus doux son sourire divin?
> N'allez-vous pas aussi vous promener ensemble
> Au fond des bois fleuris, sur le sable argentin?
> Et dans ce vert palais, le blanc spectre du tremble
> Ne sait-il plus, le soir, vous montrer le chemin?
> Ne vois-tu pas alors, aux rayons de la lune,
> Plier comme autrefois un beau corps dans tes bras?
> Et si dans le sentier tu trouvais la Fortune,
> Derrière elle, en chantant, ne marcherais-tu pas?

> Hast thou not once again, now, a young mistress fair?
> And when falling asleep with her soft hand in thine,
> Do not memories vague of thy bygone despair
> Make her sweetest of smiles appear still more divine?
> Dost thou not walk again, as in faraway days
> With her tread silver sand, 'neath the flowering trees?

And the spectre-light poplar that bends to the breeze
Does it not in that palace green point out your way?
Dost thou no longer hold, in the moon's silv'ry light,
Another soft body that yields in thine arms?
And if on the path, Fortune beckoned you, bright,
Wouldst thou not follow after it, singing her charms?

He would and indeed did sing to keep his courage up, choking back the sobs that rose in his throat, as in spite of his good fortune and laudable intentions the sinister image of his dark love once again overwhelmed his mind. The comparison in *La Nuit d'Octobre* between Aimée and George reveals all too clearly how much more powerful was even the memory of his former passion than the actual enjoyment of his present liaison. He was so grateful to Aimée; he longed to be *in love* with her as well as to love her. But within a few months the attempt to do so was driving him back to despair— and the depths into which he sank whenever he sought oblivion.

In January he wrote her a letter revealing all he was suffering; he admitted having relapsed into his former 'stupidities'—a mild term to describe the debauchery—nights of endless whoring, gambling and drinking—to which he had again given way. He did not ask her forgiveness, only her understanding:

I love you and you are worth far more than I am. But try to imagine, my dear, what I am feeling. For the past eight days I have been in an unendurable state. You know it, it is appalling, and not even worth pitying, for it is my own fault. . . . Think how much disgust, how many regrets, torments of every kind bring about such a condition. . . . I am dropping with fatigue, I have an irresistible urge to escape from myself for a few hours and to sleep peacefully in some loving arms; I cannot do it, I am chained to my work, but I will call you as soon as I can.

Even God was invoked: 'Pray to whatever God you wish,' he wrote to her, 'and ask him to teach me to make you happy.' For both Aimée and Caroline Jaubert were devout. Alfred longed to, but could not share their faith. He could do no more than hope in God; and expressed his thoughts and feelings in a magnificent poem, *Espoir en Dieu*, which alternates between despair and stoicism. Believing Christians terrified him, yet atheism repelled him. His reason was in revolt against the faith from which his heart so desperately needed to take comfort. Yet he proclaimed with as much firmness as any believer that prayer was a cry of hope; that for God to answer us, we must turn to Him, that those who suffered would be forgiven.

Unfortunately, Aimée d'Alton's letters to Alfred have been lost, but we know from his to her that she continued to love him even when, as now, he did not conceal from her either his vices or his weaknesses. One would give a lot to know in what words Aimée suggested to Alfred that they should get married. Her motive was certainly unselfish, sincere and good; for not at any time during their affair did she show herself in any but the very best light. Yet sex appeal is a mysterious quality and there are few men of Alfred's type to whom a difficult conquest of a frigid yet passionate mistress would not appear more exciting than the loving surrender of a compliant adoring young girl. There is a good deal of evidence that Alfred simply became bored by poor Aimée after the few months of happiness he had known with her. He gradually saw less and less of her. Had there been no other reason for his refusal permanently to link his life with hers, this would have been enough.

He explained the other reasons to her in some detail. For one thing, neither of them had enough money on which to set up a suitable establishment. Gaily he pretended to admit that if she had had a million he would have laughingly accepted and would have written a sonnet about it whilst smoking a cigarette:

> You see that it is not false pride that restrains me. My conscience would in that case be clear, and I do not doubt that I would have enough time and strength to return everything to you in due course.

He then dropped the persiflage and continued on a more serious and sincere note:

Cartoon by Alfred de Musset, from his sketch-book illustrating the courtship of Pauline Garcia by Henri Viardot:

Indiana (George Sand) proves to Madame Garcia that
the less money a man has, the more eager one should
be to give him one's daughter in marriage

Cartoon by Alfred de Musset, from his sketch-book illustrating the courtship of Pauline Garcia by Henri Viardot:

Alfred on his sick-bed, with Sister Marceline and Paul

I am too weak for such great resolutions; if I took them I would be untrue to myself; I should be heroic for a fortnight, then my courage would vanish and my security; any small misery or foolishness would drive it away, and then what would happen? Having tried to be strong and brave, I would only have been vile. . . . It would literally be a crime to drag you after me. Not only an illness or a sudden death might make me break my promises, but health, mental repose, confidence, might make me do so. Your letter made me afraid for you, for I suffer so much that my heart could not restrain itself from leaping at the thought of such a hope; however, I have not hesitated an instant, thank God! I would be horrified at myself if I took advantage of you.

And when Aimée would still not take his refusal as definite he begged her not to go over the same ground again:

It is not amusing, either for you or for me. I am wrong, if you like, but I cannot change myself. Please be kind and do not bring the matter up again. I would not have the courage to answer again and to go over everything that is in my mind.

Every argument Alfred brought up was correct. He would certainly have made Aimée unhappy. Neither she nor possibly he would have minded, had she been able to make him happy. That was beyond the power of any woman to do. By the age of twenty-six he irrevocably equated love with suffering. He had in fact grown to want it that way. They gradually drifted apart. How much suffering their separation caused Aimée is merely a matter of speculation. It is a matter of fact that she never loved another man. In 1861, after Alfred's death, she did get married—to Paul. As his wife she was able to share for the rest of their joint lives in the cult of the one human being whom they had both adored more than any other on earth.

J

ᗎᗎᗎ IX ᗏᗏᗏ

Supper with Mademoiselle Rachel

I

A<small>T WHAT</small> precise moment Alfred became bored by Aimée
is relatively unimportant. It can be stated with certainty,
however, that by the end of 1838, although he was still seeing
her, his interests were more than slightly engaged elsewhere.
Another 'dark lady', another legendary figure in her own
right, had already begun to claim them.

Meanwhile, the lovely Pauline Garcia—sister of La
Malibran and herself also a fine singer—had appeared as a
concert artist and made her operatic debut as Desdemona
in Rossini's *Otello*, a version of Shakespeare's tragedy more or
less contemporary with Verdi's, but much less powerful. In
doing so Pauline had not feared to challenge comparison in
this part with the performance of her late sister, a fact which
naturally increased the interest of the Parisian public.

Alfred had met Pauline at Madame Jaubert's, and was
considerably attracted by her. She had many admirers, and
did not respond to his personal homage, although no doubt she
was flattered by his high regard for her artistic gifts. On
1 November Alfred published in the *Revue* a long and eulogistic
article on her operatic début. Even so, his admiration and his
desire to please the lovely Desdemona, did not exceed his
integrity as a music-lover and critic:

> . . . It has been said that . . . Mlle Garcia surpassed La
> Malibran. That is saying a great deal and taking matters
> at great speed. One does not surpass perfection. Each of us
> tries to attain it according to our gifts, and only a very
> small number succeed in doing so, but among those
> privileged beings to whom it is from time to time permitted

to attain to supreme beauty, I cannot understand why comparisons should be made. Anyone who can hear and who listens has the right to say, 'I prefer this performance', but never the right to state, 'this is a better one'.

The general tone of the article was, however, extremely laudatory.

At the same time another star who had engaged Alfred's critical approval to an even higher degree was rising on the Parisian scene, at the Comédie-Française.

Pauline Garcia had given a concert on which Alfred had written another long article, which appeared in the previous January. It contained the following passage:

The very same day on which I had heard Mlle Garcia, in the morning, crossing the Pont Royal, I had met Mlle Rachel. She was in a hired cab with her mother, and as they drove along, she was reading, probably studying a part. I watched her as she drew nearer, her book in her hand, with her sweet and serious expression of deep preoccupation; she glanced at her book, then seemed to reflect. I could not avoid making a mental comparison between these two young girls, of the same age, both destined to make a revolution and inaugurate a period in the history of the arts; one, knowing five languages, accompanying herself with the ease and confidence of a master, full of fire and vivacity, talking like an artiste and a princess . . . singing like her sister; the other, knowing nothing except to read and understand; simple, reserved, silent, born in poverty, and having as her only possession, her only occupation and her sole glory, that little book that fluttered in her hand. And yet, I said to myself, they are sisters, those two children who do not even know one another, who may never meet. . . . One has only to open her lips for all the world to love and admire her, one might say that she was born like a flower, with music for her perfume; but the other, what work, what effort that little head must make in order to understand the subtlety of a courtesan of Louis XIV, the nobility and modesty of Monime, the untamed soul of Roxane, the grace of the Muses, the poetry of passion!

How difficult is her task, and what a prodigy if she succeeds in it! . . .

Rachel was to exceed even Alfred's hopes for her but as he so touchingly wrote, not without terrific struggles, which undermined her precarious health, for she was tubercular, and led to her early death. She would undoubtedly have become the greatest star of the French stage and possibly, according to all accounts, the greatest actress the world has ever known, without his championship. Yet at that time she was still far from the height of her fame and Alfred was certainly among the very first French critics to recognize her incipient genius.

There were others who were more reluctant to do so. One of them, M. Jules Janin, had also praised her talent but when Alfred became Rachel's champion M. Janin retracted his earlier eulogies and reverted to somewhat sharp criticism. A journalistic duel now ensued between them. The debate aroused interest and amusement among their readers and was, of course, of enormous publicity value to Rachel. She was grateful to M. de Musset and when, one evening after her performance in *Tancrède*, they met accidentally in the Palais-Royal, she invited him to her home, to supper.

Alfred subsequently wrote an account of this party in the form of a letter to Caroline Jaubert which was published among his posthumous works. He sent it to her in return for a letter from Pauline Garcia that Madame Jaubert had forwarded to him and as one good turn deserved another, 'I shall serve you,' he wrote, '*A Supper with Mademoiselle Rachel*, which will amuse you if we are both still of the same opinion and if you still share my admiration for this sublime girl.'

Rachel had been accompanied home by several of her friends but in due course they gradually drifted away.

'. . . Rachel noticed that she had left her rings and bracelets at the theatre, so she sent her maid to fetch them. So there was no servant to prepare the supper! But Rachel got up, went out to change, and into the kitchen. A quarter of an hour later she returned in her dressing-gown and nightcap, with a scarf around her neck, pretty as an angel, carrying a plate on which there were three beefsteaks which she had cooked herself. She put the plate down in the centre of the table, saying to us: 'Enjoy yourselves.' Then she went back to the kitchen and returned, carrying in one hand a tureen full of steaming soup and in the other a saucepan containing spinach.—Here's the supper! —no plates nor spoons, for the maid had gone off with the keys. Rachel opened the sideboard, found a salad bowl full of salad, took the wooden fork, unearthed a plate and began to eat.

'But,' said her mother, who was hungry, 'there are tin spoons and forks in the kitchen.'

Rachel went and fetched them, handed them out to her guests. Here began the following dialogue, in which you will see that I have altered nothing:

THE MOTHER: My dear, your beefsteaks are overdone.

RACHEL: You're right, they're as hard as wood. In the days when I used to run our household I was a better cook than that. So that's one talent the less. It can't be helped; on the one hand I've lost, but on the other I've gained.— Aren't you eating, Sarah?

SARAH: No, I don't eat with tin forks.

RACHEL: Oh! So since I bought a dozen silver ones with my savings you can't touch tin any longer? If I get any richer you'll soon want one manservant behind your chair and another one in front of you. (Lifting up her fork): I shall never banish these old forks from our house. They've served us too long, haven't they, Mama?

THE MOTHER (her mouth full): What a child she is!

RACHEL (to me): Imagine it, when I was appearing at the Molière theatre, I only had two pairs of stockings and every morning . . .

At this point her sister Sarah started mumbling in German, to prevent her from continuing.

RACHEL (continuing): No German here!—It's nothing to be ashamed of.—Well, I only had two pairs of stockings, and in order to appear in the evening I had to wash one pair every morning. They were hanging up to dry on a string in my room, whilst I wore the others.

MYSELF: And you did the housekeeping?

RACHEL: I got up at six o'clock every morning and at eight o'clock all the beds were made. Then I went to the market to buy the dinner.

MYSELF: And did you shake up the basket to turn a penny or two?

RACHEL: No, I was a very honest cook, wasn't I, Mother?

THE MOTHER (still eating): Oh yes, that's true.

RACHEL: Only once, for a month, I was a thief. When I had spent four sous, I reckoned five, and when I'd spent ten sous, I reckoned twelve. At the end of the month, I had three francs in hand.

MYSELF (severely): And what did you do with those three francs, Mademoiselle?

THE MOTHER (as Rachel kept silent): Monsieur, she bought herself the works of Molière with 'em.

MYSELF: Really!

RACHEL: Well, yes, I did. I already had a Corneille and a Racine; but I had to have a Molière as well. I bought it with my three francs and then I confessed to my crimes.

. . . The servant returned, bringing back the forgotten rings and bracelets. They were put on the table. The two bracelets are magnificent; they must be worth at least four or five thousand francs. With them was a golden crown, also of great value. The whole lot lay around on the table, together with the salad, the spinach and the tin spoons. During that time, remembering the housekeeping, cooking, bed-making and weariness of her poverty-stricken past, I looked at Rachel's hands, rather fearing to find them ugly or worn. They are charming, white, well-shaped, elongated as spindles, real princess's hands.

Sarah, who was not eating, continued to grumble in German. It was interesting to know that during the morning she had been involved in some escapade or other, too far from the maternal wing, and had only been forgiven and allowed to take her place at table at her sister's repeated requests.

RACHEL (in answer to the German grumbles): You're boring me. I want to tell the story of my youth. I remember that one day I wanted to make punch in one of those tin spoons. I held my spoon over the candle and it melted in my hand. By the way, Sophie, give me some kirsch. We will make punch. Ouf! that's enough supper.

(The cook brought a bottle.)

THE MOTHER: Sophie's made a mistake. That's a bottle of absinthe.

MYSELF: Give me a little of it.

RACHEL: Oh, I would be so pleased if you would take something with us!

THE MOTHER: They say that absinthe is very good for one.

MYSELF: Not at all. It's very bad, and detestable.

SARAH: Then why did you ask for some?

MYSELF: To be able to say that I had something, here.

RACHEL: I would like to drink some.

She poured some absinthe into a glass of water and drank it. She was brought a silver bowl, into which she put sugar and kirsch; then she lit her punch and made it flame.

RACHEL: I like that blue flame.

MYSELF: It's much prettier when there are no lights.

RACHEL: Sophie, take away the candles!

THE MOTHER: Certainly not! Certainly not! What an idea! Really!

RACHEL: It's intolerable! . . . Sorry, dear mother, you are good, you are sweet (she kisses her), but I want Sophie to take away the candles.

One of the visitors picked up the two candlesticks and put them under the table.—Twilight effect.—The mother, green and blue turn and turn about, in the light of the punch, fixes her gaze on me and watches my every movement.—The candles are put back again.

The punch was ready. Rachel filled all the glasses and served her guests; she then poured the remainder of the punch into a hollowed plate and began to drink it with a spoon, then she took my walking-stick, drew out the dagger it contained and picked her teeth with the point of it.— At this moment the vulgar chatter and childish talk ceased. One word sufficed to change the entire scene and to allow poetry and artistry to appear.

MYSELF: How well you read that letter, to-night. You were deeply moved.

RACHEL: Yes, it was as if I felt something in myself breaking. . . . But all the same, I do not like that play. [*Tancred.*] It's false.

MYSELF: You prefer the plays of Corneille and Racine?

RACHEL: I like Corneille, although he is sometimes trivial and sometimes bombastic.—All that is still not the real truth.

MYSELF: Oh! Slowly, Mademoiselle.

RACHEL: Look—when in *Horace*, for instance, Sabine says:

'One may change one's lover, but not one's spouse,'
Well, I don't like it. It's coarse.

MYSELF: You will at least admit that it's true?

RACHEL: Yes. But is it worthy of Corneille? Talk to me about Racine! That one I adore! Everything he says is so beautiful, so true, so noble!

MYSELF: *À propos* of Racine, do you remember having received an anonymous letter some time ago, giving you some advice regarding the last scene in *Mithridate*?

RACHEL: Perfectly; I followed the writer's advice and since then I have always been applauded in that scene. Do you know the person who wrote to me?

MYSELF: Very well. It was the woman with the most wit and the smallest foot in the whole of Paris. [An obvious reference to Madame Jaubert.] What role are you studying, now?

RACHEL: This summer we are going to play *Mary Stewart*; then *Polyeucte*, and perhaps . . .

MYSELF: Well?

RACHEL (striking the table with her fist): Well, I want to play *Phèdre*. They tell me that I am too young, too thin, and a hundred other nonsensical things. But I answer: That is the most beautiful part in Racine; I intend to play it.

SARAH: My dear, you may be wrong.

RACHEL: Leave me alone! If they think that I am too young and that the part is not respectable, *parbleu!* I've said worse when I played Roxane; and what did it matter to me? If they think that I am too thin, I maintain that's ridiculous. A woman who nurtures an infamous love and who is dying rather than give way to it; a woman dried up by fire, by tears, a woman like that would not have a chest like that of Madame Paradol. It would be a contradiction. I have read the part ten times during the past eight days; I do not know how I would play it, but I feel it. The newspapers may talk, they will not put me off it. They do not know what to invent, to harm me, instead of helping and encouraging me, but if necessary, I'll play it to four people. (Turning towards me): Yes, I have read certain articles full of frankness, of conscientiousness, and I do not know anything better, more useful; but there are so many who use their pens to lie, to destroy! They are worse than thieves or murderers. They kill the human spirit with pinpricks. Oh! I would like to poison them!

THE MOTHER: My dear, you never stop talking; you'll tire yourself. This morning you were up at six o'clock, I don't know what was itching you. You have been chattering all day and you've been acting to-night; you'll make yourself ill.

RACHEL (vehemently): No; leave me alone. I tell you, no! It makes me live. (Turning to me): Would you like me to fetch the book? We will read the play together.

MYSELF: If I would like it! . . . You could not suggest anything that would give me greater pleasure.

SARAH: But my dear, it is half-past eleven.

RACHEL: Well, what's stopping you from going to bed?

Sarah thereupon went to bed. Rachel rose and went out; in a moment she returned, carrying the volume of Racine; her air and movements had something solemn and religious

about them; she was like an officiant proceeding to the
altar, carrying the sacred utensils. She sat down next to me
and trimmed the candle. The mother settled down,
smiling.

RACHEL (opening the book with deep respect and bend-
ing over it): How I love that man! When I get my nose into
this book, I could stay like this for two days, without
drinking or eating!

Rachel and I now began to read *Phèdre*, the book
on the table between us. Everyone else went away. Rachel
gave a slight bow to each one as they left, but went on
reading. She first recited in monotonous tones, as if it were
a litany. Little by little she became animated. We exchanged
remarks, our ideas, on every passage. She finally reached
the declaration. Then she stretched her right arm out on
the table; her forehead resting on her left hand, leaning
on her elbow, she abandoned herself completely. She was
still only speaking in semitones. All of a sudden her eyes
sparkled—Racine's genius lit up her features, she went
pale, then flushed. I never saw anything so beautiful, so
interesting; never, in the theatre, had she made such an
impression on me.

Fatigue, a slight hoarseness, the punch, the lateness of
the hour, an almost feverish animation on those little cheeks
framed by her night bonnet, some kind of incredible charm
that flooded her whole being, those brilliant eyes that
consulted mine, a childish smile that somehow managed
to slip into all that; everything, even the table heaped up
in disorder, the trembling flame of the candle, her mother
dozing beside us, all of it composed a picture worthy of
Rembrandt, a chapter of a novel equal to *Wilhelm Meister*,
and a memory of the life of an artiste that will never
fade from my mind.

By this time it was half-past twelve. Her father returned
from the Opera, where he had seen Mlle Nathan make her
début in *La Juive*. No sooner had he sat down than he
spoke two or three most brutal words to his daughter,
ordering her to stop reading. Rachel closed the book,

saying: 'It's revolting, I shall buy a night-light and read alone in my bed'. I looked at her; two big tears flowed from her eyes.

It was indeed revolting to see such a creature being treated like that! I rose and went away full of admiration, of respect and tenderness.

And on returning home I have hastened to write you, with the accuracy of a stenographer, all the details of that extraordinary evening, thinking that you would keep them and that one day they would be found again.

2

Alfred was not mistaken and fortunately this enchanting piece has for all time preserved the scene. It is known that the evening he described so delightfully was that of 29 May 1839, when Mlle Nathan had made her début at the Opera and *Tancrède* had been given at the Théâtre-Français. Rachel was then eighteen years old. She had had a miserable childhood, dragged up and all over the Continent by her wretched father, a Jewish pedlar, little better than a beggar. When she became rich and famous her family continued to exploit and prey on her.

Rachel did not achieve her ambition to appear as *Phèdre* until four years later, in January 1843. No other actress, either before or since has, by all accounts, surpassed her in this most difficult role in French dramatic literature.

After she had read the part to him Alfred was aflame to write a tragedy for Rachel. It was to be based on a subject taken from French medieval history, and to be called *La Servante du Roi*. Rachel was, at first, almost as enthusiastic about it as the author. She invited him to stay, that summer, in the villa at Montmorency where she was living with her family. In a letter to Madame Jaubert he immortalized Rachel again, in a thumbnail sketch of one sentence:

How pretty she was the other evening, running about her garden in *my* slippers and a little knitted black and red woollen bonnet.

But Rachel's interest in the poet and his drama was more business-like than sentimental. One or two scenes of it were written, in alexandrines in the classical style. She received them enthusiastically and recited them at private parties. But she was determined to appear in Racine's tragedies before committing herself to performing *La Servante du Roi* at the Comédie-Française. Arguments and disputes arose between them and finally Alfred abandoned the play, unfinished. There was never a complete breach, yet when they did occasionally meet in later years their attitude towards one another was friendly but cool.

Alfred wrote a poem as an epitaph for his unfinished play which he addressed but never sent to Mademoiselle Rachel:

> . . . Cette langue de ma pensée,
> Que tu connais, que tu soutiens,
> Ne sera jamais prononcée
> Par d'autres accents que les tiens.
>
> Périsse plutôt ma mémoire
> Et mon beau rêve ambitieux!
> Mon génie était dans ta gloire;
> Mon courage était dans tes yeux.
>
> Those words that thou hast said,
> Those inner thoughts of mine,
> Will ne'er be spoken, now,
> By other lips than thine.
>
> Though my memory should fade,
> And my fine dream in fragments lies,
> My genius lay in your fame
> And my courage in your eyes.

❧❧❧ X ❧❧❧

Aftermath of a grand passion

I

PARIS, IN 1839, contained a galaxy of men of talent such as has rarely been assembled either in that brilliant capital or any other.

Among the greater writers were Hugo, aged thirty-seven; Balzac, forty; Lamartine, forty-nine. There were Alfred de Mussett and Alfred de Vigny, and also the lyrical but political poets-in-exile, the German, Heinrich Heine, who became a Parisian by adoption, and the Polish patriot, Myckiéwicz. Ingres, the great neo-classical painter, was the oldest among these geniuses, fifty-nine; Delacroix, the romantic master, was forty-one. The musicians included Rossini, then forty-seven; Berlioz, perhaps the greatest and certainly the unhappiest and most neglected at thirty-six; the brilliant young Liszt, aged only twenty-eight, most famous European concert pianist, and Frédéric Chopin, another Polish exile, who in the previous December had left Paris for Majorca with his new mistress, George Sand.

Rachel and Dorval were queening it in the theatre, and even in the underworld of gambling hells and brothels there was at least one young woman who dared to dream of riches and fame. Moreover, her dream in due course came true.

She was only a little more than sixteen at the time. Her name was Céleste Vénard. She achieved notoriety as La Mogador, although later she insisted on calling herself (with every legal right to this title) the Comtesse Lionel de Chabrillan.

Céleste was a nineteenth-century Manon Lescaut. Her childhood was appalling, although at that period unfortunately far from unique. Her mother's lover attempted to seduce

her. She left home, starved, and was befriended by a prostitute,
Thérèse. Swept up in her company by the police, the child,
aged about fourteen, was 'educated' in the women's prison of
Saint-Lazare. There she met a girl Denise, whom after her
release she re-joined, in a brothel. At the age of sixteen she
too became a registered prostitute. In due course Céleste
married her des Grieux, the Vicomte de Chabrillan. She became a theatrical star, theatre proprietor, dramatist, novelist,
and was nicknamed 'the poor man's George Sand'. She did not
wait until her old age to write her *Mémoires*, but first published
them in 1854. In them she drew a vivid picture of her dreadful
childhood and youth, for her literary facility was not very
inferior to George Sand's. If she was bitter and took advantage of her powers of self-expression to work off certain ancient
grudges, this was not unnatural. She was at least honest and
straightforward, not in the least self-righteous, although
perhaps not always strictly truthful. The episode to be related,
however, is generally accepted as an accurate description of a
strange encounter:

> My fall had neither changed my character nor tamed
> my pride. . . . During my stay in this house of ill-fame I
> had occasion to display these qualities when I met there
> a man whose glory, although great, barely suffices to
> make one forget his evil-living. . . .
> The first time I met him . . . I was in a pretty bad
> temper; it is difficult for me to describe the impression he
> made on me.
> I was sent for. I followed Fanny into the small salon.
> A man was sitting by the fireplace with his back to me.
> He did not even take the trouble to look at me. His hair
> was fair; he was thin and seemed of medium height. I
> took a few steps forward. His hands were white and slender;
> he was drumming on his knees with his fingers.
> I stood in front of him; he raised his eyes. He was more
> of a spectre than a man. I looked at that premature ruin,
> for he seemed to be barely thirty, in spite of the lines in
> his face.
> 'Where do you come from?' he said to me, as if he
> were awaking from a dream, 'I don't know you.'

I did not answer; he began to swear.

'Will you reply, when I do you the honour to address you?'

My face flushed and I said:

'Do I ask you who you are, or where you come from? Am I obliged to give you a birth certificate before meeting you? Well, I haven't got one.'

He continued to look at me with his bewildered expression. 'Stay here,' he said, 'I wish it.'

I listened to no more and went out.

I ran to tell the fat woman what had happened. She shrugged her shoulders and told me I was wrong, that that gentleman was her best friend and that he sometimes stayed with her for eight days at a time, that he was his own best recommendation and one of the greatest men of letters of this century.

'That man!' I exclaimed, astonished.

'That very man.'

'Well, then, I'd advise him to write less well and to talk better.'

Denise was there and bent over to whisper in my ear:

'She's crazy about him because he has a lot of money, but he's a nasty man, brutal, dishonest and always drunk. I'm sorry for those who are unlucky enough to catch his fancy.'

A violent ringing of the bell made the whole house shake.

It was my enemy who was angry because I had left him alone.

'Don't go back,' said Denise.

'On the contrary,' I replied, looking ironically at the fat woman, 'I don't mind having a close look at a great genius. One can always learn something from educated people.'

I went back to the little salon.

'Ah! so you've returned,' he said to me. 'In this house everyone obeys me; you will do the same.'

'Perhaps.'

'There's no "perhaps" about it, and to begin with, I want you to have a drink with me.'

He rang; Fanny came running.

'Drinks!' he said.

She returned with three bottles and two glasses.

'Well, what would you like? Rum, brandy, or absinthe?'

'Thank you, but I only like coloured water, and I'm not thirsty at the moment.'

He swore like a Templar, and having filled his glass with absinthe he drained it.

'Your turn, now, or I'll beat you.'

He filled two glasses and brought me one, swaying. I watched him come towards me, a little frightened by his threat, but determined not to give in. I quietly took the glass he offered me and threw the contents into the fireplace.

'Oh,' he said, taking my hand and making me twirl around, but without hurting me, 'you are disobedient, so much the better . . . I like that just as well. . . .'

He took some gold pieces in one hand, a full glass in the other:

'Now drink,' he repeated, 'and I'll give you these.'

'I will not drink.'

'Oh!' he said, laughing and leaning over a little, 'what a charming character, as impervious to fear as to self-interest. Never mind, I like you like that. Come and sit down on this sofa and tell me your story.'

I sat down without speaking.

'You've been unhappy and persecuted, haven't you? I bet that like your companions, you're at least a general's daughter. Tell me, frankly, do you like me?'

'I dislike you intensely.'

'Then you're not like the others. They're all mad about me, or at least they say so. But what would you? One cannot control one's sympathies. I can't bear them, but you seem original to me and I like you. Take this gold! You haven't earned it, but I give it to you. Leave me. Go away!'

I hastened to take advantage of my dismissal. . . .

I had so often repulsed him that he could no longer do without me. He came to see me two or three times a day. . . . It exasperated me.

'What do you want, now? Why do you insist on seeing

(*Archives of the Comédie-Française*)

Alfred de Musset by Eugène Lami (1841)

Madame Allan-Despréaux

me? The sight of you simply disgusts me. If it is during your nightly orgies that you compose such lovely things as I read this morning, I'm sorry for you, for by next day you must be unable to recognize their author, and that's a pity. It's a fine thing for you to despise women and hold them in contempt. You're less than debauched; you're nothing but a drunkard. If one woman made you unhappy, that's no reason to condemn all the rest of us. Perhaps you're right to despise us, but in that case, why not leave us alone?'

I was a little afraid of the effect this violent harangue might have on him. He listened to me at the beginning, staring at me with haggard eyes, but I was soon reassured for when I finished speaking I saw that he had fallen asleep in his chair . . . I went out on tip-toes.

It appeared that he bore me no ill-will, for next day he asked permission to take me out to dinner. Madame promptly agreed, without even mentioning it to me. . . . He came to fetch me at six o'clock and took me to the *Rocher de Cancale.*

I was very simply dressed, in a frock and hat I was wearing for the first time. I was pleased with my clothes; I felt a little less depressed, perhaps because for the second time I was allowed out of that horrible house.

In the first moments I had nothing much to complain of, except a few jokes in bad taste, not very kind in any case, for which I reproved him as best I could.

The waiter serving us brought a bottle of soda-water.

One might make a thousand guesses before discovering the crazy idea that now occurred to this man, who had chosen me as the victim of his caprices. He took the soda-water syphon as if to pour himself out a drink and turning it towards me, he drenched me from head to foot.

At a certain age and in certain circumstances one might have regarded it merely as a bad joke; but I was so unhappy that I was exasperated by this sudden pretence of folly. I shed a torrent of tears, but they were tears of rage.

The more I cried, the more he laughed. If I had remained another moment in that private room I would have broken his head, no matter what the consequences.

K

Fortunately for Alfred, herself and posterity, Céleste took to her heels. With all her versatility, she did not apparently count a sense of humour among her assets. She never forgot nor forgave this incident, which was undoubtedly a sorry exhibition of horseplay.

Her description of their first meeting and of this unfunny practical joke show in the harsh light of realism what Alfred meant when he wrote so ashamedly to Aimée that he had once again given way to his 'stupidities'. Even Céleste recorded that he had only wanted to talk to her, that he made her a present of gold pieces and never did her any worse harm than give her new dress a drenching. True Frenchwoman that she was, she had been most deeply shocked to find a man of his genius in the low brothel where she worked. She had read his verses, and between the lines of her contemptuous words were reluctant admiration and pity. And she spoke truly when she told him that he was no vicious debauchee but merely an unfortunate alcoholic.

Prosper Mérimée (who nevertheless remained Alfred's devoted friend and was instrumental in securing his election to the Académie Française) described another occasion, when with a party of friends they visited a brothel together. They had all been drinking and Alfred suggested that they should go there with him and watch him kiss a prostitute in the light of twenty-five candles. They accepted with pleasure but when the moment came Alfred, to their considerable disappointment, passed out.

'Think how much disgust, how many regrets, torments of every kind bring about such a condition', he had written to Aimée. When the inner tensions became insupportable he would take refuge in the brothel from the torments of life outside; it was a flight from reality into a state of semi-torpor and temporary forgetfulness. But no real escape lay in that direction.

2

It would have been surprising had the publication of the *Nuits* not drawn some response from George. It may well have been the terrible denunciations in the *Nuit d'Octobre* which decided her to publish a new edition of *Lélia* in 1839. She had revised it during the winter of that year when, with Chopin and her children she had spent two ghastly months in the Monastery of Valdemosa, in Majorca. The gaunt half-empty old stone building was deathly cold and it rained incessantly. The local inhabitants, scared by the presence among them of a consumptive (for they thought the disease contagious) and scandalized by this woman who traipsed all over their wild mountains in man's clothing, refused to sell them food. Chopin's racking cough grew worse every day. Finally they managed to return to France. George Sand has been over-rated as a novelist, but underestimated as a journalist. She was a brilliant descriptive writer. Her *Letters d'un Voyageur*, some of them from Venice addressed to Alfred, others to Franz Liszt, and her *Un Hiver à Majorque* still remain among the best travel books ever written.

But in the revised version of *Lélia* her style was as highfaluting, the passages as purple as ever. In this she expurgated the references in the first edition to the heroine's frigidity, but added several new pages in which the hero, Sténio, now became a caricature of Alfred in his cups. He was described in horrible terms, compared to which Céleste's 'harangue' seems milk-and water. He had dissipated the fruits of his genius. His verses now merely adorned the albums of society women. Working up her rhetoric into a furious diatribe, George continued:

Down there, a wild spectre is howling in a tavern. What do they call him, now-a-days? Lift up your trembling arm, O spectre! Raise to your soiled lips the onyx cup of the bacchante. Drink, defying her, the health of Lélia. Blame that madly proud woman who despises the charming lips and perfumed hair of so handsome a young man. For soon Sténio will be nothing more than a vessel into which are poured the fifty-seven different wines of the Archipelago.

The words 'madly proud woman' were a direct quotation from the *Nuit de Décembre*.

Ah! faible femme, orgueilleuse insensée.
Malgré toi, tu t'en souviendras!

George had indeed remembered. Yet her pride was as implacable as ever; her reply as self-righteous:

Lélia has not been struck by lightning because a man has cursed her. Her heart still belongs to her, and that heart encloses the consciousness of the Divine, the intuition of love and of perfection. Since when has one lost sight of the sun because one of the atoms which its rays had set on fire has disappeared into the shadows?

3

The happy sequel to the *Confession* which Alfred had told Aimée would be inspired by their pure and tender love remained unwritten.

Those gold pieces which he so generously gave away to little whores with whom he had no wish to sleep, and others that he threw away nightly on the gaming tables, were emptying his purse at an alarmingly rapid rate. He had from time to time obtained advances on his future contributions from the *Revue des deux Mondes*. He did his best to earn them by writing articles and short stories, for which he was being pressed by their representative, who was constantly calling on him for copy. Alfred revolted against this 'pot-boiling'. He complained to Paul that he was being made to work like a literary galley-slave.

He decided to write another novel, a sequel to the *Confession*, but sadly different from the happy story he had promised Aimée. Once again the subject was partly autobiographical. The hero was to be a poet whose inspiration, under the strain of an unhappy love affair and financial stringency, gradually petered out. He was finally to perish in an Alpine disaster.

When Paul asked him what he was writing, Alfred answered:

Later on you can tell me what to call it. It is not an autobiography because the story is not entirely my own, nor a novel, for I am writing in the first person singular.

There is too much fiction for it to be a confession, and too many true things for a mere tale. It's a work without a title. Unfortunately, what is only too true, is the unhappiness which has made me write it and the tears I have shed in doing so.

It was this work, finally entitled *Le Poète Déchu*, that Alfred had been writing when George published the revised version of *Lélia*. It was never finished.

In the middle of one night, Paul thought he had seen Alfred creeping into his bedroom on tiptoe, a light in his hand. He moved so quietly that Paul did not wake up completely. The next morning, however, he remembered the incident. He went to a certain shelf in his bookcase on which he kept a box of duelling pistols. It had disappeared. Fortunately Paul had locked the ammunition in a drawer of his desk and it was still there.

Whether Alfred had intended to commit suicide on that night of despair is doubtful. Next morning he received Rachel's invitation to spend a few days at her country house, which immediately revived his interest in life. A week or two later he went to stay in the country with another friend. Presumably during that summer his mind was preoccupied with the tragedy he was working on for Rachel, for he published nothing in the *Revue* between February and October. On the first of that month a poem entitled *Idylle* appeared. It was cast in the form of a duologue between two young men, Rodolphe and Albert, discussing their respective mistresses over a supper party. It was a minor variant on the Coelio-Octave theme, of no great consequence.

4

The *Nuits* had been written during 1835 to 1837. The revised version of *Lélia* came out in 1839. Yet whilst in poetry and prose the lovers of Venetian days had been pouring out their emotions—Alfred, his sorrow, his bitterness and his resolve to forgive although he could never forget; George, her vitriolic portrait of the debauched Sténio—they were, during those same years, carrying on a very friendly and at the beginning even affectionate correspondence.

Alfred's letters have unfortunately been lost but George's remain to reveal another strange facet of their dying relationship. She was clearly most anxious to get back those passionate love-letters she had written to him after she had sent Pagello home to Italy, and particularly her *Journal Intime* in which she had given rein to her despair at the time when Alfred had refused to see her. Immediately on arriving at Nohant after their final rupture in the spring of 1835 she had had a violent bilious attack. As soon as she recovered from it she set about obtaining a separation from her husband, Casimir, together with the right to the sole possession and administration of her property. She had become the mistress of Michel de Bourges, the lawyer whom she had engaged to fight her case for her.

When they parted Alfred had offered to return her letters to her but she had not then wished to take them. But in December 1836 she wrote to him twice on the subject. For it appeared that Madame de Musset had 'with incredible imprudence' shown one of George's notes to Alfred to various friends, which had given rise to 'ignoble comments':

> I cannot think without bitterness that the saddest cries from my heart, my mind's most ardent words, the most vivid pages I ever wrote, should remain in the hands of a person who hates me, to be delivered up to public ridicule. . . .

This long and gently reproachful missive ends—perhaps with intentional irony:

> Adieu! May your muse ever be your dearest mistress, as she is the most beautiful and most worthy of you!— Think of me sometimes as of a brother in his tomb.

From George's next letter, written on 15 December, it appears that Alfred naturally resented the aspersions she had cast on his mother. She told him that his letters to her were at La Châtre, in the safe keeping of a woman friend whom she trusted. Some time during that month George and Alfred seem briefly to have met. There is a bald and cynical reference to such a meeting in the diary of Charles Didier, on 27 December. He was then George's lover, but their affair was of short duration, for she found him a bore, although a handsome one, and he had no confidence in her:

> She told me that she had seen M. and that she felt herself completely cured. That is how passions end. She had to arrange something about her letters, and there was nothing more than a conversation, during which she was struck by his narrowmindedness.

By the spring of 1837 George was again living at Nohant. This time her lover was Maurice's tutor, Mallefille, of whom, poor fellow, she made a complete fool when she began her affair with Chopin under his nose a year later. George had apparently asked Marie d'Agoult to recover her letters to Alfred for her but nothing came of this suggestion.

Alfred had apparently written to George again in April 1838, for on the 19th of that month, when she was once more in Paris with a view to meeting Chopin, she wrote to him very tactfully and even affectionately:

> I did not very well understand the rest of your letter. I do not know why you ask me whether we are friends or enemies. It seems to me that last winter you came to see me and that we spent six hours together in fraternal intimacy, after which we should never doubt one another, even if we neither saw nor wrote to one another for the next ten years . . . and in truth I cannot possibly imagine why or how we would deceive one another at present. . . .
>
> If you would like to come and see me it would make me very happy. If you do not want to, I shall not be in the least offended. . . .

Alfred does not appear to have accepted this 'fraternal' invitation. It seems that at that time he had some reason, or imagined he had, to suspect George's motives. There was no further correspondence between them until August and September 1840. By that time their mutual antagonism had deepened. George's letter, dated 31 August, was written after her return —with Chopin and the revised *Lélia*—from Majorca. Her tone was still just friendly, but formal. She now addressed him no longer in the affectionate second person singular, as *tu*, but as *vous*:

They are at Nohant, in a box of which I have the keys here. I will write at once to Papet to send me this box and as soon as I have received it I will inform you so that you may come and fetch them, if that is still your intention.

When you were so ill last winter I cursed this story of these letters of four years ago. You must have understood why I did not come to see you, if during that dreadful trial you thought about me. I do not have to tell you that for my part I thought a lot about you.

G. S.

There is no record of 'Sténio's' thoughts on receiving the above note. The final communication was brief and business-like:

Friday [September 1840]

The letters have arrived. If you wish to come and fetch them you will always find me in between five and six o'clock in the afternoon.

George

If you do not want to come (which would be very bad) I will send you old Rollinat to make the exchange. Let me know what suits you best in this respect.

No reply from Alfred is recorded. But he had taken Caroline Jaubert fully into his confidence, and sent her a note:

At the moment of writing my suggestions for this exchange, I thought of you.—Will you be at home this Thursday morning?—I will bring you the portfolio, that you can read at your leisure, and then you can advise me— knowing the facts.

Whether Alfred was aware of it or not, Madame Jaubert made copies of George Sand's letters. Matters continued to drag on for another two years. On 24 November 1842 Alfred wrote to Caroline that nothing had yet been done about this exchange of letters. In the end, George's friend, Gustave Papet, took charge of them. He returned her *Journal Intime* to her, but a copy of it remained in Madame Jaubert's possession. Alfred never got his own letters back from George.

In the winter of 1840 Alfred's health broke down. For weeks he was seriously ill with pneumonia. In September of that year he went with his brother to spend a few weeks with their friends, the Berryers, at their château, Augerville. Their way there led through the forest of Fontainebleau, where six years previously, in 1834, Alfred and George had spent so many romantic nights. He had never returned there since. Paul feared the effect on his health of re-visiting those scenes, 'those deep shades, those spinneys tall as Gothic cathedrals, those dark hills against a fiery sky'. Alfred did not speak and did not appear to be suffering too deeply from the memories that woodland setting invariably recalled. But after ten days he left his brother, Caroline Jaubert, and the rest of the house-party at Augerville, and returned to Paris alone.

One evening six months later—in February 1841—after all those years of separation he unexpectedly met George again, at the Théatre des Italiens. He left the theatre and rushed home. Once more, as in 1835 and 1836, the Muse was awaiting him. The candles were lit, her place at his table was laid, and he sat down to write throughout the night. By next morning he had finished the poem that was the last in the series begun in *La Nuit de Mai*, the epitaph of his grand passion and one of the loveliest of all. It was entitled *Souvenir*.

The poem began by describing in long, rolling stanzas of the tenderest lyrical beauty the scene in the Forest of Fontaine-bleau that had been the setting of his youthful love. The poet reaffirmed his belief in love's supremacy. Then, in lines as dramatic but no longer as bitter as those of the *Nuit d'Octobre*, he described his meeting with his former love, his only beloved, for ever the most dear, who had now become 'a whited sepulchre, a living tomb, in which floated the dust of our dead love'. She was still young and beautiful, possibly even more beautiful than in the past, but her eyes, her smile, her voice, were no longer the same. Yet his heart was still filled with her past image. He could at that moment have gone to her and cried: 'What, oh faithless one, have you done with our past?' but he saw that an 'unknown woman' had taken possession of that voice and those eyes, and he let 'that cold statue' pass him by. But even although lightning struck him dead, even if like a sailor he were to perish in the tempest, he would never renounce the memory of that greatest love of his life.

This exquisite *Souvenir*, this supreme testament to love, ended with the famous verse:

> Je me dis seulement: 'A cette heure, en ce lieu,
> Un jour, je fus aimé, j'aimais, elle était belle.
> J'enfouis ce trésor dans mon âme immortelle,
>   Et je l'emporte à Dieu!'

One could forgive George Sand almost anything for having inspired that *Souvenir*.

⫸⫸⫸ XI ⫷⫷⫷

'My strength and life have gone from me . . .'

I

In the winter of 1840 Alfred was just thirty years old, an age at which most young men are approaching their maturity. He had not been an infant prodigy. His talent had not begun to develop until he was in his late teens. But during his twenties it had reached to the highest point it was to attain. His greatest poems were written under the pressure of intense and unhappy emotion. The pressure of such emotion and even more probably the effects of the remedy he sought for his inner tensions had taken toll of his health and strength. He was not—and could he have been a great poet if he had been?—capable of taking life easily. He was, to quote Goethe, '*Himmelhoch jauchzend, zum Tode betrübt,* invariably either raised to heavenly heights of joy or plunged into the depths of melancholy. In psychological terminology, he was manic-depressive. Under the influence of alcohol he might either play wild and silly pranks, as when he had drenched poor Céleste's dress with soda-water, or attempt suicide, as Paul recorded.

For many years his high spirits were genuine and when he took part in the gay stag parties organized by Tattet and his other fashionable men friends, he was the gayest and maddest of them all. Now, however, he became more and more conscious of the fact that even such wild parties could no longer distract him and after one of them he told Paul: 'I did my best to amuse myself like the others; but I only managed to get fuddled, for I have lost my capacity for enjoyment'. He tried nevertheless to recapture the gaiety of past years. After having indulged in a series of late nights he caught a chill, which developed into pneumonia. A very high temperature is one of the usual

169

symptoms of this illness but Alfred's delirium seems to have
made an unusual impression on those who nursed him.

He was, as he had always been, an appalling patient. His
doctor, mother, sister and brother were at their wits' end to
control him. One morning, half-delirious, he insisted on getting
dressed, determined to go to the baker's to buy himself some
bread, because he claimed that they were starving him to
death. Fortunately, Madame Jaubert arrived during this
minor crisis. She firmly ordered him back to bed; he obeyed
her and became calmer as she stroked his forehead with her
tiny hand. His old friend, the Duchesse de Castries came to sit
with him, and also a younger, equally aristocratic lady, the
Princesse de Belgiojoso. He informed her plaintively that he
was dying, to which she replied: 'You can be reassured about
that; nobody ever dies in my presence.'

Alfred was apparently not too ill to respond to those com-
forting words from a very pretty woman. After she had left,
promising to visit him again, he said that he had no intention
of dying that day.

When he became better he began to take an interest in the
hallucinations caused by his fever. He described them to Paul,
who later recorded one of these half-sleeping, half-waking
visions:

It was then the middle of March. The sun was shining
on his work-table in the centre of his room, at that time
covered with medicine bottles . . . but he saw it as it had
been when he had taken to his bed, with all his papers
and books, the inkwell and the pens symmetrically arranged.
Soon four little winged genii picked up the books, papers
and inkstand, and having cleared the table placed on it
the medicine bottles in the order in which they had arrived
from the chemist's. When he saw the famous Venetian
medicine, which his doctor, M. Chomel, had allowed him
to take, the invalid greeted it with a wave of his hand in
the Italian manner, murmuring: 'Once more Pagello
has saved my life. . . .' From the midst of the ranks of
medicines there now arose a bottle of champagne, with its
stopper of gold foil; it was mournfully borne off on a

stretcher by two of the little genii. The convoy now proceeded up a path that wound into the distance. Down
another path came a carafe with a crystal stopper, garlanded with roses, sliding gently down the slope whilst the
little genii strewed flowers in its path and the medicine
bottles formed a guard of honour.

After this ceremonial entry the carafe doffed its crown
and modestly took its place on the overmantel. The genii
. . . removed the unwanted medicine bottles and put things
back as they were, preparing his work-table for the poet,
now recovered. . . .

Alfred also told his doctor, M. Chomel, about this experience, to which the good-humoured reply was: 'You had a
genuine attack of poet's pneumonia. It is certain that you
will never be like anyone else, either in sickness or in health.
But try to benefit from the advice you gave yourself. The
apotheosis of the water carafe is not enough; you must also
remember that nature has provided the daytime for staying
up and the nights for sleeping.'

'That aphorism,' Alfred answered, 'is less profound than
those of Hippocrates, but I'll promise to think it over.'

It is extraordinary that most of Alfred's French biographers
have completely missed the significance of this incident. They
nearly all regarded his little phantasy of the genii as another
symptom of his mental unbalance. It was, in fact, conclusive
evidence that he was very much in control of himself. There
was always method in Alfred's madness. On this occasion he
had indulged in nothing more sinister than a form of rather
charming wishful thinking. 'Little genii' who tidy up for people
are a common folk-myth, from Ireland to Germany, from
leprechauns to *Heinzelmännchen*. But the sub-conscious
motivation of the phantasy is obvious. As soon as he was once
again ill, his subconscious reverted to memories of his Venetian
illness, of George and Pagello. On his return home he had
brought Pagello's prescription with him, and Pietro had written
to him, five years previously:

When you find yourself surrounded by a dozen bottles of
champagne, remember that tubful of water and gum arabica

that I made you drain at the Hotel Danieli, and I am sure that you will have the courage to fly from them. . . .

He had not had that courage (but how he wished that he had) and if there were in reality kind little genii to bear away the alcoholic poison and replace it with a carafe of water, prettily crowned and garlanded with roses, how easy a way out of his guilt-complex that would be! And he replied to Dr. Chomel as flippantly as he had to Pagello to whom he had written that never again would he drink that accursed liquor—without deeply reproaching himself.

Nothing is so restful to an alcoholic as an illness during which temptation is removed by those nursing him, nothing so genuine as his remorse during that period of enforced sobriety, nothing so fleeting as the resolutions he then makes and which he knows he will break as soon as he is on his feet again, when the carafe of pure clean water will remain unused on the over-mantel, as he returns to his work-table and his indispensable poison.

2

During the worst period of his illness a nursing nun was engaged by Madame de Musset. She was Sister Marceline. Whether during his bad nights she ever heard her patient murmur the name of George is not known, for she was the essence of discretion as well as kindness. To Alfred she seemed a saint. When he was convalescent he composed some touching verses that expressed his gratitude, his deep admiration for this Sister of Mercy. But he absolutely refused to write them down:

'Those verses,' he told Paul, 'were for myself, alone; they concern only myself and I owe them to no one. Surely I have the right to compose a dozen stanzas for my private use and to recite them to myself when I wish to. I will say them to you just once; try to remember them if you can.'

Paul could only remember four of those verses later on:

> Pauvre fille, tu n'es plus belle.
> A force de veiller sur elle,
> La mort t'a laissé sa pâleur.

En soignant la misère humaine,
Ta main s'est durcie à la peine
Comme celle du laboureur.

Mais la fatigue et le courage
Font briller ton pâle visage
Au chevet de l'agonisant.
Elle est douce, ta main grossière
Au pauvre blessé qui la serre,
Pleine de larmes et de sang.

Poursuis ta route solitaire.
Chaque pas que tu fais sur terre,
C'est pour ton œuvre et vers ton Dieu,
Nous disons que le mal existe,
Nous dont la sagesse consiste
A savoir le fuir en tout lieu;

Mais ta conscience le nie.
Tu n'y crois plus, toi dont la vie
N'est qu'un long combat contre lui,
Et tu ne sens pas ses atteintes,
Car ta bouche n'a pas de plaintes
Que pour les souffrances d'autrui.

The first line of this poem is somewhat belied by a drawing
Alfred made in the series of brilliantly funny cartoons illustrating the courtship of Pauline Garcia by M. Viardot. In these
he represents two of her rejected suitors, the sculptor Barre
(who was afterwards to sculpt the bust of Alfred on his tomb
in the cemetery of Père Lachaise) and himself. He had not
then grown a beard but had a small drooping moustache, the
wispy down-flow of which he deliberately exaggerated to
emphasize his own comic despair at his rejection by the
young lady. This particular drawing, made like the others
during his convalescence to amuse himself and his friends,
shows Alfred reclining supinely in bed during his illness. Paul,
very smart and handsome, offers him a large syringe with
which to wash away his physical and emotional troubles.
Behind Alfred's bed stands Sister Marceline, crisply coiffed,
calm and gentle. She has large dark lovely eyes and looks like a
slighty idealized version of George Sand. Whether she in fact

did look like that or not, she was according to this cartoon
still very pretty. She was also intelligent. She brought Alfred
through his illness, and during his convalescence they had
many conversations. He believed firmly in God, but had not
since his childhood been a practising Catholic. Sister Marceline
naturally did her utmost to bring him back into the fold and
in his love and admiration for her he seems to have promised
her that on his recovery he would once more perform his
religious duties. She embroidered him a silken feather, on which
were the words 'Remember your promises', and also knitted
him some woollen mittens. Seventeen years later, on his
instructions, these trivial mementoes were buried with him.

He firmly believed that she had certain clairvoyant powers
and this view seemed shortly to be confirmed. One of the causes
that had brought on his breakdown was his constant worry
about his financial obligations. He saw no hope of bringing his
affairs into some order. This kind of mental distress was also,
as George Sand had written to Buloz in 1835, one of the
symptoms of his Venetian illness. The *Revue des deux Mondes*
had made him considerable advances on his future contributions, but work as he might, he never seemed able to pay them
off. When he was convalescent, however, a publisher, Charpentier, decided to bring out a collected edition of his poems. It
sold very well and for the time being solved all his financial
problems. Charpentier continued to publish both his verse and
prose works. Triumphantly Alfred informed Paul more than
once: 'Marceline had predicted it to me and yet that poor
Sister does not even know what a line of verse is!'

Sister Marceline was unable to nurse Alfred in his later
illnesses, but kept in touch with him and came to see him
from time to time.

At the end of March he wrote in excellent spirits to his
godmother:

> At present I am enduring the most boring part of an
> illness. I made the mistake of recovering, so that I am no
> longer regarded as an invalid and at the same time have
> not the strength to behave like someone who is well. . . .
> But I have, nevertheless, good grounds for feeling at peace;
> my affairs, which had been worrying me are improving,

Alfred de Musset by Landelle (1854)

Alfred de Musset's statue outside the Comédie-Française

although slowly. My good intentions are firmer than ever. I only need a little strength and a ray of sunshine to improve this bad weather. . . .

In June he went to the country, to stay with Tattet. But although his physical health was restored he could not overcome the depression he had been feeling before his illness. Instead of joining Tattet and his fellow guests on their gay riding parties as in the past, he would ride off alone up some silent forest glade. One morning when he had not joined them but had gone out by himself they went into his room to look for him. On the table lay a poem entitled *Tristesse*, one of the most famous he wrote:

> J'ai perdu ma force et ma vie,
> Et mes amis et ma gaîté,
> J'ai perdu jusqu'à la fierté
> Qui faisait croire à mon génie.

> Quand j'ai connu la Vérité
> J'ai cru que c'était une amie;
> Quand je l'ai comprise et sentie,
> J'en étais déjà dégoûté.

> Et pourtant elle est eternelle,
> Et ceux qui se sont passés d'elle
> Ici-bas ont tout ignoré.

> Dieu parle, it faut qu'on lui réponde;
> Le seul bien qui me reste au monde
> Est d'avoir quelquefois pleuré.

> My strength and life have gone from me,
> My friends and my gaiety,
> Not even my pride has remained
> That faith in my genius sustained.

> When first of Truth I learned,
> I thought I had found a friend,
> When I understood it, I spurned
> With disgust that lesson's end.

L

Yet it lives eternally,
And those who have scorned its worth
All else have missed on earth.

God speaks, and one must reply;
All that I in this world have kept
Are the tears I have sometimes wept.

⤗⤗ XII ⤙⤙

Princess Charming?

I

THE KIND Duchesse de Castries, like the other ladies who
had so devotedly hovered around Alfred's sick-bed, had
hoped that the good influence of Sister Marceline would last
and that he would find comfort in religion for his real or
imagined sufferings. The Duchesse had written him to this
effect from Dieppe, where she had been spending the summer.
Alfred wrote her a long, affectionate and sincere reply:

> I consider that I have the right to say that I am bored,
> because I know very well why. You tell me that what I
> lack is faith . . . not only have I faith in many and excellent
> things today, but even were I to be deceived I do not
> think I would lose it for that reason.
>
> As regards *higher things* and the faith of Sister Marceline,
> I can say nothing. Belief in God is innate in me; dogma
> and practice are impossible for me, but I do not want to
> justify myself in any way . . . I will tell you what I am missing
> now—something much more mundane. . . . I find myself
> high and dry, like a fish in the middle of a cornfield, but
> I have never been, am not, and never shall be able to live
> alone, nor to agree that to do so is to live at all. I would just
> as soon be an Englishman. That is all my trouble . . . so-
> called women of the world seem to me to be acting in a
> comedy without even knowing their parts. On the other
> hand my lost loves have left certain scars behind that
> cannot be cured by some namby-pamby ointment. What
> I need is a woman who is something, anything; either
> very beautiful or very kind or in the last resort even very
> wicked; very witty or very stupid, but something.

The same refrain once again; Alfred could not live without love, was only half-alive unless he was in love and when he wrote that letter he was only saying in prose what he had so often expressed in poetry.

So that it was not surprising that very shortly after having done so he found, or thought he had found, another woman on whom to concentrate his yearnings and who appeared to possess all the qualities he had listed, even to the stupidity.

Among his glamorous visitors had been the Princesse Belgiojoso, whom he had met several years ago at Madame Jaubert's. She was one of the stars of that fascinating semi-aristocratic, semi-artistic, semi-intellectual set that also included George Sand from time to time, and the beautiful blonde Comtesse Marie d'Agoult, who had returned to Paris from Italy in the previous autumn with her three illegitimate children by Franz Liszt, the second of whom, Cosima, then a mere tot, in due course married Richard Wagner.

The Princess and the Countess were intimate enemies, devoted rivals, who detested one another. Marie was fair, with a superb figure; Christine, small, dark, with the pure oval face and regular features of a Leonardo da Vinci angel. Both were heiresses, both had made unhappy marriages. Both dabbled in politics and aspired to run artistic-cum-intellectual-cum-political *salons*.

Christine, born in Milan in 1808, was a passionate patriot and adherent of the anti-Austrian movement, the *Risorgimento*. Like Marie she was extremely well educated and was married at sixteen to a man, the Prince Emilio Belgiojoso, with whom she had nothing in common except their devotion to the future independence of their country. He had been the lover of Byron's famous Italian mistress, the Countess Guiccioli and very soon after their marriage returned to her. Christine who was as fearless as George Sand and an excellent rider and shot, t rew herself wholeheartedly into politics and became a follower of the great nationalist leader Mazzini. In 1831, she was compelled to leave Italy on account of her romantic political adventures and arrived in Paris as a refugee.

She was very quickly taken up by those French men of letters and politics who admired her country's struggle and even more this lovely feminine embodiment of it. One of her admirers was Adolphe Thiers, another the historian François Mignet, member of the Académie Française, who became her lover and gave her *salon* the necessary weight and distinction to rank as one of the most important in Paris. But Christine did not disdain lesser conquests. Among her admirers was Franz Liszt. When he reluctantly came to visit Marie in Paris in 1840, only to find, with some relief, that she was ill in bed, he spent most of the few weeks he stayed there flirting with the Princesse de Belgiojoso. In their conversation and correspondence Marie and Franz scathingly referred to her as *La Comédienne*—the actress, and not without truth. But unlike the other society ladies described by Alfred in his letter to Madame de Castries, Christine did know her part—in his case only too well.

She was not particularly interested in poetry and had no appreciation whatever of Musset's genius. In this she was unfortunately not unique. For she was an intellectual snob and took her opinions from the eminent Frenchmen she admired. Alfred had long ceased to impress his contemporaries as anything but a literary lightweight; even Sainte-Beuve was no longer loyal to his earlier belief in him. Alfred came into the lowest of all the Princess's categories; he was neither a political nor an artistic but merely a social conquest. His reputation as the most romantic lover of his day was, however, still considerable and it flattered Christine that this no longer very young, yet handsome and attractive man, who adorned many brilliant *salons*, including her friend Caroline Jaubert's, should now appear to adore her.

Marie d'Agoult was a shrewd psychologist and in spite of their mutual antipathy hardly exaggerated when she described the Princesse de Belgiojoso as a heartless coquette. Christine was a practised flirt. Her type of beauty was not dissimilar from George's. She, too, had thick raven hair, dark eyes which appeared to hint at an inner passion, a very white skin and a charming figure, with the sloping shoulders so greatly admired in her day. Marie's friend Henri Lehmann, a second-rate artist who had a fashionable following, painted her wearing a crown of water-lilies. It was an apt choice on her part for there was something nymph-like in her appearance and a watery coolness in her blood. She was very devout; her confessor, the

Abbé Coeur, was a fashionable priest of the day. Her *salon* was furnished in the style of a Gothic oratory, hung with silver-flecked black velvet, and several skulls were included among her bibelots.

It was not until after his illness and the end of his affairs with Aimée d'Alton and Rachel, when he was feeling so desperately in need of falling in love again, that Alfred began to pay court to the Princess. As usual Madame Jaubert was his confidant and he kept her informed of the progress—or rather the lack of it—of their relationship. A story was told about it which in view of Christine's parade of moral rectitude seems surprising.

The Prince de Belgiojoso did not live with his wife but was also a member of that gay circle of dandies and men-about-town to which Alfred belonged. They had known one another for years and were on excellent terms. On one occasion Alfred had apparently induced the Princess to have lunch with him in a private room at a fashionable restaurant known as the *Cabaret du Divorce* at Montparnasse. Her husband had given a rendezvous to another lady at the same restaurant and when he happened to hear that Musset was upstairs with an unknown charmer, he, according to Léon Séché, went up to find him and to suggest that they make a foursome together. Musset only managed to stave off the Prince after a good deal of trouble. As soon as he had been safely seated in another room his wife took to her heels. This anecdote seems more in line with a Feydeau farce than with Christine's allegedly serious character.

Whilst she resisted any attempt at greater intimacy on Alfred's part, she played with his affections, alternately blowing hot and cold. His letters to Caroline at this time are plaintive:

> I held her hand, I kissed it for a whole minute, and she let me do so. I told her a hundred times that I did not want to make an easy conquest of her, that my *amour-propre* was not in the least involved, that I only wanted a word of friendship from her to be happy for a whole day. She believed me and she saw that it was so. . . .

She invited him to stay with her at Versailles, when

. . . she kept me there for eight days, at every moment avoiding the opportunity to talk to me, treating me like a stranger. She can only have had three reasons for that: either she did not trust herself, which I do not believe; or else she made me suffer for her own amusement, knowing that she ran no risk in restoring my peace of mind; or else she was behaving coldly, with pride and indifference, which is what I believe. Well, that is wicked and hateful. . . .

Things went from bad to worse. At table, Alfred happened to make a joke which annoyed Christine, although Caroline had not apparently found the same pleasantry in the least offensive. They quarrelled over a game of chess, which he had lost,

. . . when she saw that she was making me dreadfully unhappy, so then she beat me over the head with her charming smile between her two dimples, and glances that were enough to give me a headache. . . . And can you imagine that person (I can certainly not tell you her name) who forbids me to drink unwatered wine under the pretext that I am coughing, and who pins a plaster on my heart with a hundred thousand pinpricks!

He was writing half in self-pity, half in self-mockery and it would be a mistake to take these complaints too seriously. Such trivial incidents were no evidence of any grand passion, which Christine was incapable of feeling and therefore of inspiring. Had Alfred not at that time been so deeply miserable and depressed he might not have wasted more than two years in dalliance with her.

Yet although he had told her that his *amour-propre* was not involved and that no more than a platonic relationship between them would be enough to make him happy—a little more tenderness than friendship, a chaste affection rather less than love, after a year or two this was no longer strictly true. He was by then acutely conscious of the fact that he was no longer as young nor as attractive as in the past; he was hag-ridden as well, by his secret awareness of his poetic decline. The pinpricks of which he had complained had by then become feline scratches and were beginning to sting.

Christine had no sense of humour but she did have a very strong appreciation of her own beauty. One of the accomplishments that made Alfred so popular in the *salons* of his friends was his ability to draw in a few minutes a brilliant and sometimes cruel caricature of one or the other of his fellow-guests. At a party given by Madame Jaubert, Christine had claimed that it would be impossible to draw a caricature of her, as her features were 'too regular'. Alfred rashly accepted the challenge. In a few light strokes he set down those features, emphasizing the slight droop of her dark, sentimental eyes, the provocative turn of her shoulder. Their friends crowded around to admire this delicately malicious sketch. Christine gave it a disdainful glance:

'It has something . . .' she murmured reluctantly as she handed it back to the artist and then turned away.

'Now you have burnt your boats,' Caroline whispered to Alfred.

He declared to her in vain that he had never found Christine more attractive than when he had made that drawing. He had omitted to write this tribute underneath it and the harm was done.

Finally, in October 1842, Alfred took a startlingly cruel revenge for all the coldness and unkindness that Christine had shown him. He pilloried her publicly in one of the most scathing poems ever written by a rejected poet about a former love. This was no light, pencilled caricature, but a full-length portrait etched in acid of an empty-headed and hypocritical *poseuse*, whose measure her disillusioned adorer had now completely taken. (It must have given great pleasure to the Comtesse d'Agoult.)

If Night in the dark Sistine chapel was beautiful [he declared] then she, too, was beautiful. If goodness consisted in giving charity whilst feeling no pity, then she was good. If to think consisted of speaking in a soft, gentle voice, she could think. If prayer meant no more than lowering to the ground or raising to Heaven a fine pair of eyes, then she, too, prayed. If a bud that had never opened could flower in the passing breeze, she might have smiled. If the cold hand on her heart had ever felt on its human clay the dew of Heaven, she might have wept. Had not pride, like the useless lamp shining by a coffin, shone over her empty heart, she might have loved. She was dead but she had never lived and from her hands had fallen the book that she had never read. This poem was dedicated to the Princess and was entitled *Sur une Morte*. To the malicious delight of all their friends and acquaintances Alfred sent it to the *Revue des deux Mondes* where it was published. It was a very good poem.

Christine did not immediately see it, for she happened not to have read the copy of the *Revue* in which it appeared. But everyone else did. A witty comment on the situation was made by one of Alfred's later biographers, Maurice Donnay: 'Had a visitor's book been opened in . . . the *salon* hung with black velvet and silver "tears", and had all those who had recognized the Princess signed it, it would have been filled with signatures.'

When Christine did read it, she cleverly informed her friends that it referred to Rachel, with whom Alfred had recently quarrelled. Others were allowed to believe that the subject was George Sand. But the cold contempt in every line of *Sur une Morte* is as far removed from the lyrical melancholy of *Souvenir* as was this trivial, time-filling affair from the greatest passion of Alfred's life.

Madame Jaubert did not spare Alfred but gave him a thorough scolding for this inexcusable lapse of taste. It was unnecessary, for almost as soon as *Sur une morte* had appeared he bitterly regretted having published it. He was laid up again, either with bronchitis or influenza, and wrote to her:

> . . . Whilst I have lain as stiff as a stick under fourteen blankets, perspiring great drops and coughing hard enough to break the windows, I was thinking about my last verses, and sincerely regretted them, very sincerely. . . . On my word of honour, I do not love her any longer, at least, I do not suffer two sous' worth when I think of her . . . but I am not happy; I would like to find some means of repairing the damage . . . I do not want a reconciliation, no further *rapprochement*. Now that it is finished, I have had enough. But I feel that I went too far, and I would like to leave a better impression. . . .

And he wrote to the Princess, expressing his regret frankly and honestly. She replied very sharply indeed, for which she was certainly not to be blamed. Her letter was not preserved; according to Alfred it was 'unprintable'. But he had been

> ... goaded into a rage. You do not know, Marraine, no! you cannot, cannot know to what an extent I was ... worn out, led on and let down, what depths of perverse and wicked coquetry were coldly used on a poor devil who loved with all his heart and surrendered like a dumb beast. ...

The least he could do, he felt nevertheless, was to forbid this poem from being published amongst his collected works. It did not appear in them until after his death.

2

During that winter Alfred was very much alone. Tattet had left Paris and gone to live at Fontainebleau. Paul, on whom he relied more than anyone in the world for the loyalty and understanding which were indispensable to him, had left for a holiday in Italy. Alfred missed him keenly, but was careful to write him cheerful and even gay letters, so that he should not worry about him. One of these contains a delightful vignette of Rachel.

When she had shown that she was not interested in the play he had been writing for her he had been bitterly disappointed. It was true, as the Princesse de Belgiojoso had stated, that they had quarrelled. Yet fundamentally they admired one another as artists even when they were personally antagonistic. Alfred was happy to be able to write to Paul that they had made it up:

> I had supper at Buloz's on Twelfth Night. The entire *Revue* was there, as well as Rachel. The atmosphere was somewhat frigid; it might have been a diplomatic dinner. ... Fortunately Chaudes-Aigues became tight, which broke the ice. Rachel asked me if we were still angry with one another, with such a coquettish and amiable look that I answered her: 'Why did you not look at me like that and ask me the same question three years ago? You would have

known that I never bear a grudge and our quarrel would have lasted twenty-four hours.'—She gave me an even more coquettish look than the first one, saying, 'What a lot of time we wasted!'—and we shook hands on it and made it up. Rachel invited me to go and see her and I do so every Thursday. . . .

Alfred wrote a poem in the following spring, on his brother's return from Italy. It was a light-hearted rhymed travelogue, enumerating the various cities they had both visited—Florence, Milan, Genoa, Ravenna, Ferrara. Light-hearted enough until he mentioned Venice:

> . . .
> Là mon pauvre coeur est resté.
> . . .
> Mon pauvre coeur, l'as-tu trouvé
> Sur le chemin, sous un pavé,
>   Au fond du'un verre?
> . . .
> L'as-tu trouvé tout en lambeaux
> Sur la rive où sont les tombeaux?
>   Il y doit être.
> . . .
> Il fut crédule, étant loyal,
> Se défendant de croire au mal
>   Comme d'un crime.
> Puis tout à coup il s'est fondu
> Ainsi qu'un glacier suspendu
>   Sur un abîme. . . .

Aimée d'Alton, Pauline Garcia, Rachel, Christine de Belgiojoso, none of them, nor any other woman, was ever able to mend that poet's broken heart.

❧❧❧ XIII ❦❦❦

The poet's star sets

I

AFTER *Souvenir* was written in 1841 the candles were never again lit to welcome the Muse to Alfred's table. The gulf between the inspiration of this poem and the bitterness of *Sur une Morte* written in the following year, reflects the ever-growing sense of desolation, loneliness, uselessness and frustration of all kinds that had invaded Alfred's heart.

Buloz, the only one of his contemporaries who to the very end was loyal to Alfred's genius, tried in vain to goad him into greater creative activity. He succeeded to the extent that Musset replied to him in a long and satirical epistle in verse, *Sur la Paresse*, which began by airing his grievance that he was treated like some literary galley-slave and ended with the categorical statement that it pleased him to write as rarely as he wished. He explained his motives more fully to Paul:

> 'Don't you see,' [he told him when the poem was printed on 1 January 1842], 'that I have given the reasons for my silence and that . . . when they see that my contempt is genuine and sincere, they will no longer be offended by it? Those who pretend not to know that I exist will be kind enough to notice it. . . . I have written a great deal; I have composed as many verses as Dante and Tasso. Who, devil take it, ever dared to call them lazy? When it pleased Goethe to fold his arms, who ever reproached him for dabbling too long in science? If it pleases me, I shall do the same as Goethe until I die. My Muse is mine; I will prove to the public that she obeys me, that I am her master, and that in order to obtain anything from her, it is I whom they have to please.'

His inactivity was not the cause of his bitterness, but the result of it. And truly he had good reason. A fortnight after the publication of *Sur la Paresse*, the *Revue* published an article on contemporary poets by Sainte-Beuve. They were listed by the critic in their order of merit—according to his opinion—and Alfred was placed in the middle of the third class, lumped together with undistinguished versifiers, including even some lady rhymers! To this injury Sainte-Beuve added the gratuitious insult that if this young poet would more often write satires like *Sur la Paresse*, or other 'meditations' like *La Nuit de Mai*, 'he might perhaps have a considerable chance of emerging from this group'. When Alfred read this cruelly mischievous statement he remarked to Paul, 'and thou, too, Sainte-Beuve'.

The fact that Sainte-Beuve had deliberately ignored the three later *Nuits* and *Souvenir* was due to his friendship with George Sand. He had obviously gone over to the enemy and now saw in his former 'child of genius' only the drunken and dissolute Sténio. He had in fact seen him so on one or two occasions and had feigned to pity him, 'so lost and so rotten to his very core', but to write such appalling nonsense about Musset was hardly the way to express his pity or to help him.

Paul shared Alfred's resentment to the full:

> If one looks through Alfred de Musset's poems [he wrote in his biography] it will be seen that after 1842 he did not add many further satires nor 'meditations' to them, and yet M. Sainte-Beuve completely reversed his own judgement. He placed the poet who wrote *La Nuit de Mai* among the gods—after his death, needless to say. . . .

Among the poets whom Alfred most deeply admired were Michaelangelo, whose sonnets he knew by heart, and the great Italian lyrical poet Leopardi, whose little book, he said, 'was worth a whole epic'. Alfred was revolted by the Italians' neglect of this genius, which was worse than his own treatment. He expressed his love for him in an elegy, *Après une lecture*.

He could find no consolation for his frustrations and continued to deaden his sorrows in the usual manner. His character was not changing but his bitterness and constant hang-overs inevitably led to a deterioration. He became increasingly irritable and nervous, quick to take offence and also to give it. Occasionally his former high spirits, gaiety and love of fun would return, but only for short periods. His humour turned to irony.

Even his former passion now became a subject of ridicule. In 1842, he published a charming and wicked little story, in which he made fun both of his youthful self and of George. It was called *Histoire d'un merle blanc*, the tale of a young blackbird, who was, however, an albino, and white. After having searched in vain for a mate this unhappy avian freak discovered to his delirious joy a little white female 'blackbird'—*une merlette blanche*. She was his heart's delight and what was more, a literary *merlette* into the bargain. Whilst he wrote his poems, she scratched away madly, writing novels:

> One day, when she was working with unusual ardour I noticed that she was perspiring great drops and at the same time I was astonished to see that there was a great black stain on her back.
> 'Oh, my God!' I said to her, 'what is it? Are you ill?. . .'
> She told me that it was an inkstain and that this often happened to her during her moments of inspiration. . . .
> Whilst I thus chattered and wept, my wife changed colour visibly. At every tear I shed a feather appeared, not even black, but of a worn rust-colour. (I think the dye had already come off elsewhere.) After a few melting moments I found myself face to face with a bird no longer pasty and white as flour, but identical with the most common and ordinary blackbirds.

The disillusioned bird-husband flew away and sought consolation from the nightingale:

> 'How lucky you are,' I said to him. . . . 'Rubini and Rossini are nothing compared to you . . . may I learn your secret?'
> 'Yes,' replied the nightingale, 'but it is not what you think. My wife bores me, I do not love her, I am in love with the rose . . . I sing my head off every night for her, but

she does not hear me. Her petals are closed at this hour, in her heart she is enfolding an old scarab—and tomorrow morning, when I have returned to my bed, worn out by suffering and fatigue, she will open, to let a bee eat out her heart!'

2

Alfred continued to be a law unto himself. He ignored the regulation under which he, like his fellow-citizens, was obliged to present himself from time to time for certain duties in the National Guard. In this neglect he was not unique. Many French artists and men of letters did not take kindly to such discipline, although when their country needed them they invariably rushed to defend her. In September 1843 and again in 1849 de Musset spent three days in a cell, to which he had been condemned as punishment. It was in the prison jocularly known as the *Hôtel des Haricots*, presumably because the table-d'hôte consisted mainly of bean-soup. This sentence did not depress him in the least, for the cell walls were covered with drawings and verses by several distinguished previous occupants, amongst them the artists Déveria and Gavarni. Alfred's contribution was a poem describing them, gaily entitled *Le Mie Prigioni*. It caused great amusement when it was published.

3

But these spurts of wry gaiety and witty mockery were unfortunately only occasional and superficial. He who had always lived in and in some ways for society, who had always needed conversation, company, a brilliant setting, now began to become anti-social. For weeks at a time he would disappear. We know from Céleste Mogador's evidence where he would spend those weeks, to re-appear in a state of even greater depression than when he had vanished. When he did not resort to drink and low company, he would go night after night to the Opera, for he adored music and found some slight consolation in it. When he felt in the mood, he would occasionally make a social call. But on entering a *salon* he might be either drunk or sober. It was a sad sight, to those who still admired and pitied him, to see him tottering across the room, his eyes glazed, his legs very stiff, his body held carefully erect. On one such occasion a charming young woman was heard to whisper: 'Poor boy!'

'Had I loved him,' said the famous actress, Augustine Brohan, 'how I would have loved him!' But he no longer appeared very attractive; his face was prematurely lined, he was painfully thin, and his expression was that of a man who had nothing left for which to live.

After Paul's return from Italy he was stopped in the street one day by a literary acquaintance who commiserated with him on Alfred's 'silence' but who made it clear that the reason for it was fairly obvious.

He had not seen even his beloved and loving god-mother for some time. She was well-informed about him, however, and deeply worried. She spoke to Paul, asking him to have a serious talk with Alfred. Paul for once admitted that he had not sufficient influence over his brother to induce him to reform. Madame Jaubert, whose devotion to Alfred never wavered even in his worst moments, thereupon decided to perform this painful duty herself. She asked him to come and see her and after dinner, on 13 August 1844 he did so. Paul, perhaps more relieved than he would admit, knowing that Alfred's *marraine* was assuming this responsibility, left the same night on a two months' trip to Venice. When he returned in November he asked Madame Jaubert what had happened between her and Alfred on that evening. Her reply was sorrowful, dramatic and mysterious:

'Do not ask me about it,' she answered with emotion, 'I did our dear Damis' [one of her nicknames for him] 'a great wrong. It hurt me as well. I cannot repeat to you what he told me; it would be beyond my strength. I will only tell you that he defeated me on every score; that he is a hundred times right; that his silence, his ennuis, his contempt are only too justified; that if he wanted to express them, he would make those who make it their business to blame and pity him sink into the ground, and that sooner or later his immense superiority will be recognized by the whole world. Let time do its work, and do not let us play with fire, for compared to him we are only children. When he left me' [at midnight] 'the poor boy wrote me a sonnet, which he sent me very early next morning and which brought tears to my eyes; he wanted to prove to me what he was capable of doing, as if I had ever doubted him! I am keeping those verses in my archives. One day, maybe, they will be published, and that terrible evening of 13 August will not have been wasted.'

Paul asked to see this sonnet, but Alfred's godmother was afraid of reading it, refused to fetch it, and began to talk of something else. Only thirteen years later, after Alfred's death, did she give the manuscript to Paul. It was as follows:

Qu'un sot me calomnie, il ne m'importe guère.
Que sous le faux semblant d'un intérêt vulgaire,
Ceux mêmes dont hier j'aurai serré la main
Me proclament ce soir, ivrogne et libertin,

Ils sont moins mes amis que le verre de vin
Qui pendant un quart d'heure étourdit ma misère;
Mais vous, qui connaissez mon âme tout entière,
A qui je n'ai jamais rien tu, même un chagrin,

Est-ce à vous de me faire une telle injustice,
Et m'avez-vous si vite à ce point oublié?
Ah! ce qui n'est qu'un mal, n'en faites pas un vice.

Dans ce verre où je cherche à noyer mon supplice,
Laissez plutôt tomber quelques pleurs de pitié
Qu'à d'anciens souvenirs devrait votre amitié.

That a fool should condemn me leaves me cold.
If by vulgar hypocrites I am told—
Who only yesterday shook my hand—
That to-day I'm a wastrel, I understand.

They are less my friends than the glass of wine
Which stills my pain for a moment brief;
But you who know all this soul of mine,
From whom I hid nothing of my grief,

Can you also not from injustice refrain,
So soon forgetting me, down the years?
Do not call a vice what is merely pain.

M

In this glass where my torture I'd drown, in vain,
Rather let fall a few pitying tears
That friendship owes to the bonds it bears.

Madame Jaubert never did tell precisely what Alfred had said to her on that August evening. In consequence, this sonnet and her remarks, quoted by Paul, have been variously interpreted by different commentators. All these interpretations were mere guess-work, however, and a miss is as good as a mile.

The poem makes it clear that she had reprimanded him for his alcoholism, and for having increasingly gained a reputation for rudeness and bad manners. In the first verse he expresses his contempt for those who have slandered him by spreading such stories about him; those who had shaken him by the hand on the previous day and on the following evening proclaimed him a drunkard and a libertine. In the second verse he admits frankly that such acquaintances are less his friends than the glass of wine in which for a quarter of an hour he drowns his sorrows. Then, however, he gently reproves Caroline,

Vous qui connaissez mon âme tout entière,
A qui je n'ai jamais rien tu, même un chagrin,

she who knew his inmost soul, from whom he had held nothing back, not one sorrow, how could she, too, be so unjust as to believe the same of him? Pathetically he begs her not to call a vice what is an evil, a sickness. Presumably he used those arguments when he, as she told Paul, defeated her on every point and convinced her—of what? That he was in the right to drink himself to death, as he was doing? Hardly. That he had some reason for doing so, some justification? Probably. But what this justification was, whether the slights he was made to bear by Sainte-Beuve and other colleagues, or his hopeless love for George which, clearly, was still rooted in his heart, or some nameless fear, perhaps of illness, no one has ever learned. An oblique ray of light was shed on this mysterious matter several years later by Adèle Colin, Alfred's housekeeper, if she spoke the truth.

But first of all one can confidently dismiss the assertion that has been made that Alfred was an epileptic and was intensely afraid that this fact should be discovered. Never, in any one of his illnesses, or in his hallucinatory states, did he show symptoms of epilepsy. Of hysteria, certainly, though not in the vulgar but in the scientific, psychopathic meaning of that term. His childish tempers were hysterical, and so were some of his later paroxysms, for they were always designed, although subconsciously, as a means to an end. Many of his hallucinations, as in Venice and possibly in the Forest of Fontainebleau, were undoubtedly due to alcoholism or *delirium tremens*.

George had repeatedly told him that he was mad. Although she later on strenuously denied that she had ever threatened to have him incarcerated in a lunatic asylum on that night when he had caught her writing to Pagello and had frightened her by his threats, made in a moment of understandable fury, there is no doubt that Alfred was and remained convinced that she had said she would do so unless he came to his senses. And that memory could have set up some kind of trauma, so that he came secretly to believe that George *might* have been right. He had always been tormented by the unsolved riddle of his own psychology, by his 'dual' personality, and during his attack of pneumonia in 1840 even his doctor had told him, half in jest, half in earnest, that he was not like ordinary men. He had never left home and until 1850 his mother watched over him in a state of constant anxiety, which was hardly calculated to alleviate his own.

Nevertheless, it seems unlikely that if Alfred had confessed to Caroline Jaubert that he drank because he was in some such permanent state of dread, she would have told Paul that 'sooner or later his immense superiority' would be recognized by the whole world. Superiority to whom or to what? That word could only have referred to his rivals and detractors, but not to a secret thwarted passion or anxiety neurosis. And it was striking as well as curious that she should have added that compared to him they—she and Paul—were only children, when all his life his mother, brother, Caroline herself and his men friends, such as Alfred Tattet, had regarded and treated Alfred as the boy who would never grow up.

Paul could have misquoted Madame Jaubert. Both in the biography and in his later *Vie romancée* of Alfred's life, *Lui et Elle*, he showed himself capable of suppressing or distorting unwelcome facts and substituting some pleasanter fiction for anything too starkly derogatory to his idolized brother. On the evidence it seems as if Madame Jaubert was referring merely to Alfred's superiority over his enemies and denigrators. As for the sonnet, in that Alfred does no more than plead guilty to alcoholism and ask that her friendship for him should continue to be sustained by loyalty and pity.

⋙ XIV ⋘

Fate's Last Caprice

I

ALFRED'S DEPRESSION was increased when in 1847 his sister
Hermine married and went to live in the provincial city
of Angers. His mother went to stay with her daughter, at
first for some months, but later on permanently. The family
had moved a few years previously from the apartment in the
Rue de Grenelle, to which he had so gaily invited Aimée
d'Alton, and were then installed in a much larger one at No. 21
Quai Voltaire. Alfred was very fond of his sister, who was a
good amateur pianist. In the days after his return from Italy,
when he had shut himself up in his room for weeks at a time,
he would only creep out when he heard her playing a Mozart
or a Beethoven sonata, and sit in a corner of the *salon*, silently
listening. Now she had gone, taking the piano with her.
Their mother was absent too, and the brothers found the apartment very large and empty without them.

Paul was travelling a good deal. After his first trip to Italy
he was sent on an official mission to Venice where he remained
for a year, to collect historical material concerning France's
relations with the Venetian Republic. In September of 1847,
he managed to induce Alfred to go and spend a month with
his mother and sister. Alfred needed the change, but like many
less distinguished Parisians he could not bear to stay away
for more than a few weeks from his beloved city, particularly
from its night-life—restaurants, clubs, theatres, the Opera
House and the Opéra-Comique. Although Paul was still
abroad and he had enjoyed himself at Angers he returned to
Paris after a month, which for Alfred was a long time.

On his return he was pleasantly surprised by the news that

his playlet, *Un Caprice*, was to be given at the Comédie-Française.

His bad luck in the theatre had appeared to be unchangeable. After his first failure at the Odéon in his early youth, not a single one of his plays had ever reached the stage. In 1846, Bocage, a famous actor who was then director of the Odéon (and also some years previously one of George Sand's transient lovers), had wanted to stage *Un Caprice* there. Alfred, who had never forgotten the agonies he had endured over the ridicule that had greeted his youthful effort, *La Nuit Vénitienne*, had so much feared a second failure that he refused even to attend the rehearsals. It did not come to that, because Bocage's plan never came to anything and the whole scheme was dropped.

The production of *Un Caprice* at the Comédie-Française on 27 November 1847 was due to an odd and lucky freak of fate.

Madame Louise Allan-Despréaux, who before her marriage had been a talented and popular star of the Gymnase Theatre, had gone with her husband to St. Petersburg, and was very well liked at the Russian Court.

> Admitted to the highest society [Paul wrote] she had become a woman of the great world. One day, at St. Petersburg, she was advised to go and see a piece that was being given in a small theatre, and in which was a part, that of an attractive woman, that might suit her. . . . She saw this little Russian piece, and Madame Allan-Despréaux was so pleased with it that she asked for a translation of it to be made into French, so that she could appear in it at Court. . . . The Emperor Nicholas would certainly have commissioned this to be done, had not someone familiar with French literature . . . informed Madame Allan that the play that had made such an impression on her was in fact a translation. The volume containing *Un Caprice* was freely available in St. Petersburg, Madame Allan was given a copy, and when she performed it at Court, it was acclaimed as charming.

In Paris, we knew nothing of all that. When M. Buloz, administrator of the Comédie-Française, was corresponding

with Madame Allan with regard to her re-appearance at
the Theâtre-Français, she informed him that she wished
to appear as . . . Madame de Léry. With the exception of
M. Buloz, everyone at the Comédie-Française was surprised
at her choice. No one knew where she had got hold of this
little one-act play. . . . When he returned to Paris in
October, Alfred de Musset found matters well advanced. . . .

The success of *Un Caprice* was an important theatrical
event, and its extraordinary popularity did more for its
author's reputation than any of his other works. In a few
days the name of Alfred de Musset was known in those
wider circles of the public to which poetry or books never
penetrated. The kind of boycott that had weighed on him
was lifted as if by enchantment and hardly a day now
passed in which the press did not quote his verses. . . .

Un Caprice was the playlet which Alfred had written
exactly ten years previously, when Aimée d'Alton had sent
him the anonymous gift of the little silk purse with the gold
piece in it. Madame de Léry, the leading character, was
modelled on Caroline Jaubert. It must have been a strange
and sad experience for Aimée, if she saw the play, ten years later.

Paul was not exaggerating its success. In his first-night
notice Théophile Gautier told how Madame Allan had returned
from Russia with *Un Caprice* 'in her muff'. Gautier wrote
on 30 November 1847 that

> This little piece is, frankly, a great literary event. Since
> Marivaux nothing so subtle, so witty, so quietly gay has
> been produced at the Comédie-Française as this minute
> masterpiece, which was buried in a literary review and
> which Russians in that snowy Athens, St. Petersburg, re-
> discovered in order that we should acclaim it.

Un Caprice has ever since remained one of the most
popular pieces in the repertoire. (It was last performed in
London by the Comédie-Française at the Princes Theatre
in 1959.) The *Revue des deux Mondes*, whose eminent editor
Buloz had become the administrator of the Théâtre-Français,
was raked through for the rest of Alfred's plays, which to his

bitterness had over so many years remained buried in its pages. In 1848, the Comédie-Française produced one after the other— *Il faut qu'une porte soit ouverte ou fermée, Il ne faut jurer de rien, André del Sarto.* All the leading Parisian actresses now asked Musset to write plays for them. Encouraged by this late but delightful success he produced in rapid succession, *Louison, On ne saurait penser à tout, Bettine* and *Carmosine.*

If brevity be the soul of wit, Alfred de Musset was the wittiest of playwrights. For his best pieces are among the briefest ever written, their romantic sentiments seasoned by beautifully turned, crisp dialogue. Beneath their apparent inconsequentiality there is often a subtle bitterness, resembling Noel Coward at his best. The lighthearted deliberate craziness of *On ne saurait penser à tout* has a touch of surrealism that seems to foreshadow Ionesco. The actors, to whom they gave every opportunity to shine, naturally adored them.

One of the *sociétaires* of the Comédie-Française, the actor Edmond Got, was also a talented diarist. His *Journal* contains several interesting references to the plays, in which he appeared in many supporting roles. The first night of *Il ne faut jurer de rien*, in which Got was cast as the Abbé, took place on 22 June 1948.

> . . . whilst [wrote Got] the first shots in the darkness were being fired at the Porte Saint-Denis, we nevertheless gave a brilliant first performance to a full and, my word!, amused house, of *Il ne faut jurer de rien.*
>
> In this devil of a Paris there is room for everything.

The 1848 Revolution had broken out. Lamartine, the poet and politician who had so coolly received the poem addressed to him by Alfred de Musset in 1836, was at the head of the Government. But he and his colleagues were muddled idealists, who, like the sorcerer's apprentice, had unleashed forces beyond their powers to control. On 22 June there was comedy inside the theatre, but outside it, tragedy. The barricades were up in the streets; on 23 and 24 June the starving and rioting workless who had converged on the city from the suburbs and provinces were savagely shot down by the troops under the leadership of General Cavaignac.

The Comédie-Française was closed for nearly a month.

Although Alfred was imprisoned for neglecting his duties in the National Guard when such neglect was relatively trivial, he fulfilled them punctiliously as soon as matters became serious. On 1 July he wrote to Tattet:

> I have just taken off my uniform, which I had not done since the insurrection began. I will not describe the horrors that occurred; it was too hideous. . . .
> . . . on the eve of the insurrection I had another full house, plentifully adorned with pretty women, an intelligent public . . . very good actors, in fact everything for the best. I had my evening, I took it so to speak on the wing. . . . Next day, good-bye to actors, director, author, prompter. We had our rifles in our hands, cannon-shots for orchestra, incendiarism for lighting and a public of vandals. . . . I could never have dreamed of anything like it.

3

After calm was restored the success of *Il ne faut jurer de rien* continued unabated. But the critics, including Sainte-Beuve, were still unreconciled and as spiteful as ever. Nor were all Alfred's plays on an equally high level. Got, who admired the dramatist wholeheartedly, nevertheless wrote of *Louison* which was produced two years later:

> *4 August 1850* . . . when a genius makes a mistake he does not do it by halves.

Alfred should, nevertheless, have been the happiest of men, for in addition to the recognition for which he had longed since he was twenty and which—at last—was so fully his, he was to have one more great success in love.

Louise-Rosalie Ross was born in 1810 at Mons, in Belgium, where her father was a theatrical manager. As a child actress she had been discovered there by the great actor, Talma, and taken by him to Paris to play the part of the boy Joas in Racine's *Athalie*. She then studied at the Conservatoire and made her debut at the Comédie-Française in 1826. She became the leading lady at the Gymnase, having chosen for her stage-name her mother's maiden name of Despréaux. After her marriage to her fellow-actor, M. Allan, she prefixed his name to her own. She spent ten years in Russia with him and then returned to the Comédie-Française to make her reappearance there in *Un Caprice*.

Madame Allan was a very pretty woman, with the typical Walloon gaiety and charm. She was also intelligent and as popular with her colleagues as with her public, so much so that when she died, although not a *sociétaire*, the Comédie-Française was closed on the day of her funeral.

When she met Alfred they were both thirty-seven. She had kept her looks, although by that time she was inclined to stoutness. He was deeply grateful to this delightful woman and actress for having been the cause of his late but nevertheless very gratifying success. He was all too conscious of his own faults and deficiencies and when he began to pay court to her his attitude was no longer that of the glamorous, romantic young lover bound to succeed, but deferential, almost humble.

Madame Allan's most intimate woman friend was the daughter of another famous actor, Samson. Louise made a confidant of her, and was warned against losing her heart to Musset, whose reputation as a rake was by then accepted by all Paris. No doubt Madame Allan believed herself to be telling the truth when she wrote to her friend:

> Don't be afraid. I am certainly very flattered by the attentions of M. de Musset, but as for ever surrendering to him—that is a different matter. I know his character only too well and I am pretty sure that it would only be a passing whim in his case.

But Alfred was clinging to her as to his last hope of redemption. In the spring of 1849 he wrote her a lovely and touching sonnet in which he recalled that she herself had said that one should love without deceit, shame, or lies, and which ended:

> Vous dont chaque pas touche à la grâce suprême,
> C'est vous, la tête en fleurs, qu'on croirait sans souci,
> C'est vous qui me disiez qu'il faut aimer ainsi.

Et c'est moi, vieil enfant du doute et du blasphème,
Qui vous écoute, et pense, et vous répond ceci:
Oui, l'on vit autrement, mais c'est ainsi qu'on aime.

It was to be an idyll of two middle-aged lovers, calm, peaceful and exquisite—she, still beautiful; he, the child of doubt whom she would convert to loving her thus, although he had lived so differently.

He made an almost superhuman effort to prove worthy of her love and trust. For five months he gave up drinking and low company. He wrote a three-act play in verse, *Louison*, and another *Proverbe*, *On ne saurait penser à tout*, one of his most sparkling little comedies.

Madame Allan had not yet made up her mind to accept him as her lover, nor could she, to borrow the title of this piece, think of everything. When her friend Madame Samson-Toussaint left for Brazil with her husband, she went with her to Le Havre, to see her off. No sooner had she left Paris than Alfred had a relapse. She forgave him when he confessed it to her on her return. But it confirmed her resolve to remain no more than a sincerely devoted friend to him, so devoted, in fact, that she wished to inform him of her decision as gently as possible. She was so afraid of wounding his feelings that her letter, which asked him to come and see her in her dressing-room at the Comédie, was over-tactfully worded. He interpreted it as meaning precisely the opposite of what she had intended. He called to see her during the interval between the first and second acts of the play in which she was then appearing and, she wrote to her friend subsequently, 'he gave such a start of happiness, so genuine and sincere' that it pierced her heart 'like an arrow'. When she, nevertheless, still tried to hold back, Alfred, immediately disillusioned, bitterly accused her of wanton coquetry. Louise Allan was no second Princesse de Belgiojoso, but as genuine and sincere a person as she knew Alfred to be. As soon as he had left her, angry and wounded, she hastened to write to him and immediately the performance was over, herself took her note to his house on the Quai Voltaire. She had burnt her boats.

It is not easy to explain why, in his relationship with this completely honest and sweet-natured as well as beautiful woman, Alfred should from the moment they became lovers have reproduced all the details of the pattern of his stormy affair with George Sand, fifteen years earlier. For Madame Allan had no other lover nor the least intention of taking one; there was no Pagello to come between them. His bouts of almost insane jealousy were inexcusable. The only explanation seems to lie in the trauma his sub-conscious had experienced when as a little boy he had discovered that his cousin Clélie, equally sweet and kind, had been 'unfaithful' to him. Louise Allan had no sooner given herself to him than the usual pattern was established between them. He made appalling scenes, followed by abject repentances. It was undoubtedly due to his increasing alcoholism and the irreparable damage it had by this time done to his nervous system that he suffered again from acute delirium. 'He suffers from it when he becomes excited,' she explained to her friend, 'which is due to his old and sinister habits' (a perfectly correct appreciation), 'when he has hallucinations and sees ghosts.'

Desperate, terrified that he had lost Louise, Alfred completely broke down and told the whole story to his mother. Madame de Musset was growing old. Her one and only desire was that Alfred should not lose the last chance of salvation remaining to him. But how to help him was beyond her capacity. He could not help himself. In despair, he simply vanished. For four days and nights he hid himself, no doubt in one of the brothels in which during such black crises he took refuge. Madame Allan was equally distracted. At ten o'clock on the fourth night she took a cab and went to the Quai Voltaire, and at the door she found Alfred's mother waiting to speak to her.

It was exactly fifteen years ago that another of his mistresses had called on Madame de Musset, when George had come to ask her permission to take Alfred to Italy. She had then only given it with the greatest reluctance. Now, the situation was completely reversed. With tears in her eyes the old lady begged and implored Louise not to abandon her unfortunate son, for she alone could help him.

> His mother [wrote Madame Allan] clasped my hands
> and spoke to me with touching kindness, asking me to

forgive her with all the tactfulness of a woman of the great world, and then telling me how happy she was that I loved her son, whom she adored.

It was a delicate situation for both women, since no lady could officially recognize her son's mistress as such. Louise Allan, although no society woman but an actress, was nevertheless a lady in everything but social status.

> 'Save him' [Madame de Musset begged her], 'you can do it, for he loves you deeply enough. I entrust him to you. Take pity on him and do not abandon him. Even if your clear-sightedness judges him, do not condemn him. . . .'

They decided that Madame Allan should take a country house at Ville-d'Avray, on the Versailles road, and that she and Alfred should spend the summer there. She still had faith in him:

> He must work; he still has plenty of good and charming ideas, but owing to idleness and the fatigue induced by his past life he no longer has sufficient energy. . . .

In her letters to her friend, Louise Allan reveals step by step the battle fought by a sweet and steadfast woman genuinely in love with an alcoholic. There were times when she seemed to be winning, when they would spend enchanted evenings together at her piano, when she sang to him and he read poetry to her. Then the reaction—violent scenes of jealousy made on any and every pretext, mostly imaginary. Tortured and torturing her, Alfred would disappear, reappear, beg her forgiveness. . . . True to her promise to his mother, Louise forgave him time and time again. But inevitably the strain told on her. As one reads her letter to her friend Madame Toussaint, written in October 1849, one can follow almost every stage of that agonizing situation:

> . . . Twice I have broken or tried to break this relationship. But I cannot resist his despair, his nervous attacks that bring on brain-storms, hallucinations, and delirium. . . .

His repentances are just as violent, his joy at finding me again, his gratitude, which moves me so that I return to the happiness that I wanted to give up. . . . Love intoxicates him as much as anything else . . . at certain moments sublimely, but at others almost unendurably! . . . In his brooding mind, disbelief and suspicion are linked with a procession of very bitter memories, which, taken all round, are those of an ex-libertine. I cannot stand them and then, quarrels, pardons, and reconcilations again. There! I have never seen a more striking contrast than between the two beings that live in this one man. One is good, kind, tender-hearted, enthusiastic, witty, surprisingly as naïve as a child; simple, unpretentious, modest, an exquisite artist who feels and expresses everything that is most beautiful in the most beautiful language—music, painting, literature, the drama. But turn over the page and you will see the reverse: a man possessed by a kind of demon—violent, despotic, proud, mad, hard, insultingly suspicious, blindly obstinate, selfish, blasphemous, and exulting in wickedness. Once he has mounted the devil's steed, he has to remain in the saddle until he breaks his neck. That is his nature—excessive in all that is beautiful and all that is ugly. The latter phase invariably ends in illness, after which he once more comes to his senses and repents of his bad habits. I don't know how he has survived it all so long, and has not died a thousand deaths.

This is probably the most accurate description ever written of Alfred's psychopathic personality. Madame Allan had no literary pretensions nor personal venom to unload, but loved and pitied him with her whole heart.

A little more than six months later she wrote, sadly:

I have not seen Alfred for about a month. . . . Will his absence continue? I do not know. I am doing absolutely nothing about it, and as I am not at all averse to a little peace, it may last as long as God wills. If his fickle heart returns, as has happened so many times before, as he can never see me without loving me, I shall wait to see how I shall make up my mind. . . . If it is over, it will have lasted a little less than eleven months; a fine time, you will agree; it's enough to lower my pride if I had any in such things, but far from that, I am filled with humility, which is more becoming to a character that is proud but not vain. I am trying to cure myself bit by bit of feelings and passions, seeing what they lead to. All of us, men and women alike, deceive ourselves, and it is a great mistake to imagine this or that. The human heart follows its own desires without troubling about reason, or, rather our reasons. . . .

This time their rupture was final. Louise was such a sweet and good woman that it seems impossible to defend Alfred's heartlessness towards her. At that time she was starring in the part of 'Jacqueline' in his play *Le Chandelier*. It was true that she was rather too old for the part of this pretty young wife with whom the rambustious officer Clavaroche and the romantic young clerk Fortunio are both in love, that her tendency to stoutness had increased, and her figure had become definitely matronly. During the banqueting scene Fortunio has a little song in which he describes the charms of Jacqueline:

> Nous allons chanter à la ronde
> Si vous voulez,
> Que je l'adore, et qu'elle est blonde,
> Comme les blés.

The actor Delaunay, who was playing Fortunio, was reciting those lines during rehearsal when Alfred appeared, slightly the worse for drink. At the line 'We will sing a round'—'Round as a barrel' the author interrupted him in tones which were heard—and were meant to be heard—by the entire company. This impromptu pun did not bring smiles to the faces of Madame Allan's fellow-actors, for it was in inexcusable taste and cruelly coarse.

At the end of the theatrical season Madame Allan left Paris for Algiers, thus definitely placing herself out of reach of Alfred's jibes, nervous crises, and tardy repentances. Her final letter on the subject to her friend revealed that although she still loved him she knew that this love could never again make her happy and must therefore be given up once and for all:

. . . I do not know whether it is not better to live in apathy rather than only to feel alive through suffering. If you only knew, dear Adèle, how much I have been reflecting and thinking things over during the past months! If you knew what profound contempt I feel for everyone, *without exception*; to what a degree I have been haunted by other peoples' hideous egotism. If you only knew what a change I have felt in myself; how I shrug my shoulders at myself, how I despise everything, everybody, and my own poor heart! . . .

All that Alfred had been able to share with that kind heart was his own contempt and disgust for himself and his fellow-creatures, and in doing so he had wounded it irremediably.

Louise Allan-Despréaux died a year before Alfred, at the early age of forty-six. He himself was then almost a chronic invalid and when he learned of her death he was deeply and sincerely moved. Apart from Aimée d'Alton, Louise Allan was the only really good woman he had ever tried to love. Like Aimée, she was incapable either of reforming him or making him happy. Love could provide no remedy for the sufferings of *L'Enfant du Siècle*.

Immortal

I

IN 1850 Madame de Musset left Paris permanently, to live with her daughter at Angers. The big apartment on the Quai Voltaire was given up. Paul went to live in the Rue des Pyramides; Alfred first lived in the Rue Rumfort, but moved nearer to him, to the Rue du Mont-Thabor. This apartment was conveniently situated at only a few minutes' walk from the Comédie-Française and the Café de la Régence, where Alfred in later years spent much of his leisure, always impeccably dressed, eating abstemiously a couple of cutlets, drinking not at all abstemiously, mostly absinthe. When he was in a sociable mood he would gossip with the actors and writers who stopped at his table, or play a game of chess with a friend. When he was in the grip of one of his bouts of black depression, he would sit for hours without speaking a word, drinking until the waiter summoned a cab to take him home. Then he rose and walked stiffly to the door, sustained by his growing fame and the pride that had still not deserted him. The cab drove down the Rue Saint-Honoré, turned left into the Rue d'Alger, then right, to draw up at No. 6 Rue du Mont-Thabor. It was a large solid building. Alfred's apartment on the first floor was, however, dark and gloomy. To the right of the narrow corridor were the dining-room and the *salon*, behind them a smaller room for his housekeeper. The kitchen, on the left of the corridor, was separated by the bathroom from Alfred's bedroom, which had only one stained-glass window that let in almost no light, and faced the narrow courtyard and the dingy backs of the houses in the Rue Saint-Honoré.

He was forty years old when for the first time he set up a home of his own. It was clear that he would need someone to look after him, not merely a housekeeper, but also a nurse. By then the symptoms of his heart disease had become more marked. They had first appeared after his serious attack of pneumonia in 1840, when Sister Marceline had nursed him. He had subsequently had several illnesses, including bronchitis and pleurisy.

The person chosen by Madame de Musset was Mademoiselle Adèle Colin. She was efficient, patient and kind and very soon Alfred was completely dependent on her. He had originally engaged her for three months but she remained with him for the rest of his life and like other women in a position similar to hers, she gradually acquired considerable influence over her charge. She was the one who saw him at his very worst, who undressed him and put him to bed when he arrived home incapable of doing so himself. When he travelled she invariably went with him; when he was ill or during his nights of insomnia she would sit with him for hours at a time, replacing Paul who in the past had often spent all night with Alfred. He had no secrets from her. He addressed her in the familiar second person singular. She did not overtly take advantage of the situation and took care not to overstep her place as nurse-housekeeper and confidant. But even she published a book about him after his death entitled *Dix ans chez Alfred de Musset*. And it was Adèle Colin who claimed that the following incident occurred towards the end of his life:

One night Alfred awoke suddenly from a restless sleep and asked her where he was, for he was still half-dreaming.

'At home, in your own room,' she answered him reassuringly.

'Then,' he asked her anxiously, 'I am not married?'

'No; why do you ask me that?'

'If I were married,' he replied, 'my wife, seeing that I was ill, would be afraid. She would place me under a doctor who, pretending to treat me, would drive me mad. . . .'

Once again, all those years after, he had been haunted in his dreams by George's threats. In 1851 he wrote a tragic poem entitled *Souvenir des Alpes*, one of his very last. It was in an elegiac mood and contained references to Byron, who had compared the dark pine forests on their slopes to the trees surrounding a cemetery. And it contained also a forlorn echo of the great passionate lines in the *Nuits*, a couple of short verses as splendid and tragic as he ever wrote:

Aveugle, inconstante, ô fortune!
Supplice enivrant des amours!
Ote-moi, mémoire importune,
Ote-moi ces yeux que je vois toujours!

Pourquoi dans leur beauté suprème,
Pourquoi les ai-je vu briller?
Tu ne veux plus que je les aime,
Toi qui me défends d'oublier!

2

The success of his plays did not diminish and there were still many occasions when he appeared in social or theatrical circles in seeming good health; sober, completely in command of himself, elegantly dressed and as entertaining as ever. All the successful actresses longed to appear in one or the other of his comedies. Rachel had become world-famous, had a series of rich and princely lovers and lived in almost regal luxury. She had built herself an *hôtel* (more than a house though less than a palace) in the Rue Trudon, and invited Musset to a grand banquet there. Alfred gave her his arm to escort her downstairs from the *salon* to the dining-room. The staircase was somewhat narrow, and Alfred accidentally stepped on her train. She reproved him in the grand manner which she had by then adopted:

'When one gives one's arm to a lady,' she told him, 'one takes care where to place one's feet.'
'When,' Alfred rejoined, 'one has become a princess and builds oneself an *hôtel*, one should tell the architect to provide a wider staircase.'

Alfred reminded her of the good old days, when he had supped with her and they had used tin forks and spoons. Rachel good-temperedly accepted the reminder.

'Perhaps you think,' she said, 'seeing all this luxury in which I now live, my superb silverware, that I am no longer so nice as in those days? Well, I will prove the opposite to you.'

'How so?' asked Alfred.

'By coming to see you, to ask you once again to write me a play.'

But once again, nothing came of this suggestion. He was busily writing for other actresses, notably an adaptation for the stage of his early and enchanting play—which also is still constantly produced—*Les Caprices de Marianne*, for Madeleine Brohan. Rachel wrote to him from London, reminding him of the tragedy she was expecting from him. When she returned to Paris, she found that another play of his, *Bettine*, in which Rose Chéri had appeared, had not had a great success. Rachel then cooled off and Alfred threw into a drawer the sketches he had been making for this tragedy with the remark:

'Good-bye, Rachel. It is you whom I am burying for ever in this drawer.'

This time it really was good-bye.

3

His continued success as a playwright had at last made the general public aware of his poetic talent. It had also drawn attention to him in circles which for so many years had not merely remained aloof, but had dismissed him contemptuously as a playboy and drawing-room versifier. Chiefly at the instigation of Prosper Mérimée, the illustrious members of the Académie Française—the 'Immortals'—considered electing him as one of themselves. He was not elected without opposition. But finally, on 27 May 1852, wearing the celebrated uniform of dark green braided with gold, cocked hat and sword, Alfred de Musset took his seat and according to custom gave an oration eulogizing his predecessor, M. Dupaty. Alfred, like every other French poet since his day, including another one-time *enfant terrible*, Jean Cocteau, was delighted at

acquiring this status, the highest conferable on a French man
of letters.

> A murmur of satisfaction and surprise [wrote Paul]
> arose from the elegant public, drawn from them by the
> fair hair and youthful appearance of the new member.
> He looked no more than thirty.

One can visualize Alfred in that moment of triumph.
He had retained his slender figure (in his bad moments his
friends deplored his emaciation) and although his face was
prematurely lined long before that day of glory, this belated
recognition no doubt eliminated those lines, which recorded all
his past suffering and bitterness. His hair and beard were as
full and glossy as ever. And on this great occasion there was
present, among all the lovely ladies who had come to admire
and applaud the crowning moment of their favourite poet, one
whom he had never forgoten—his cousin, Clélie, his first love,
to whom he had promised a gold-leaved edition of his poems
bound in vellum.

There can be no question that when George Sand had taken
him under her spell in 1833 and captured his heart so completely and for ever, she had done that heart an irreparable
damage from which it had never recovered. Yet it was no
whole heart that had been bared to the wounds that George
had inflicted on it. It had first known and suffered from
frustrated passion on the day when Alfred, then a little boy of
ten or twelve, had been told of Clélie's marriage. Neither his
mother, his brother nor anyone else had ever suspected in
those farwaway childhood days the wrong they had so deceit-
fully done him in first abetting and then trying to cure him of
this childish passion. Since there was no Freudian nor any
other scientific psychiatry in his day Alfred himself could
not have known that it was Clélie and not George Sand who
had first filled his innocent mind with doubt and suspicion of
women; that when in his worst moments he was so cruel to all
his mistresses, including George and Louise Allan, including
even poor little Céleste whose only best dress he had drenched
with soda-water, including how many unknown girls and
women whom he had treated with equal heartlessness—even

he himself could never have guessed for what infantile slight
and betrayal he had ever since been avenging himself. His
invitation to Clélie to attend his final academic vindication,
his official acceptance by the literary 'Immortals,' was, however, the proof (if proof were needed) that he had remembered
to make certain that she should witness his finest hour.

4

Alfred's literary distinction won him another amorous
success, of more dubious value. Louise Colet was the same age
as Alfred, forty, when she set her cap at him. She was an odd
creature, almost a caricature of George Sand. She too was
passionate to the verge of nymphomania, and a literary female.
More in the theatrical than the literary tradition she had won
the reputation of trying to 'sleep herself up' the ladder of
success. She became successively the mistress of Abel Villemain,
Gustave Flaubert and Victor Cousin, and for six months, of
Alfred de Musset. This short period was long enough, however,
to provide her with material for the novel she published two
years after Alfred's death. It was the third in the trilogy which
began with George Sand's *Elle et Lui*, continued with Paul's
infuriated riposte to it, *Lui et Elle*, and was simply entitled *Lui*.
Alfred soon wearied of her attentions and her insatiable lust
and gave Adèle Colin instructions that when next 'that lady'
called she was to be informed that he had left for the country.
It was a lamentable episode in the life of the sick poet whose
Muse was now sadly watching as his inspiration gradually
waned under the stress of ill-health.

Both Lousie Allan-Despréaux and his old friend Alfred
Tattet had died a year before and their deaths caused him great
sorrow.

During his later years he spent the summers either in the
country or by the sea. His last holiday was at Le Havre, in
1856. In the hotel there he met an English family, the Lysters.
They had two young daughters, charming and pretty girls.
Alfred had always taken pleasure in the company of such innocent
young creatures. How he would have adored Marcel Proust's
A l'Ombre des Jeunes Filles en fleur, the third section of

A la Recherche du Temps Perdu, the masterpiece of another neurotic genius.

On his return to Paris the Lysters were staying in the Champs Elysées and begged him to call on them. He hurried to do so but when he reached their door he had second thoughts.

'In Paris,' he said to himself, 'there is not that informal and intimate atmosphere that makes seaside acquaintanceship so delightful. We might imagine that we had a thousand things to talk about but when we had gone over all the little incidents and pleasures of our holidays we would realize that we hardly knew one another. There will probably be other people there, compatriots of theirs, possibly some young man hoping to marry one of them. I should only be another visitor and even an unwelcome one. Good-bye, then, to all that friendly gaiety and chattering of children . . . and would I myself be as amusing and entertaining to them as I was at the seaside? I might soon be walking home regretting a lost illusion, a delightful memory that has been deflowered. I would do better not to brush the bloom off the butterfly's wings.'

And so, anticipating the Proustian hesitations and reluctances, he refrained from ringing the bell, turned, and walked home. He never saw the two charming Miss Lysters again.

5

During his last years he was constantly in financial difficulties. One day, together with Stendhal, he amused himself by working out how much he had received from the *Revue* for his poem, *Rolla*: twenty-five centimes per line. Stendahl recalled that the English publisher John Murray had paid Byron three hundred guineas for *The Lament of Tasso*, roughly a guinea and a half per line. Stendhal was indignant, but, said Alfred, 'before getting excited about it you should consider whether a similar difference does not exist between the quality of Lord Byron's verses and mine. Perhaps I have been paid enough'. Stendhal angrily denied it.

In spite of the huge success of his plays his royalties were only moderate. The system of payment had not (and still has not) varied since 1777, when the great Caron de

Beaumarchais, author of *Le Barbier de Séville* and *Le Mariage de Figaro*, had founded the Société des Auteurs Dramatiques. Each evening a representative of this society collects from the theatres the royalties due to the authors whose plays have been given. In Alfred's time payment was made according to the length of an act and as his plays were as a rule as short and concise as they were witty, his share did not amount to vast sums. On 14 March 1851 he sent a note by his housekeeper, Mlle Colin, to Arsène Houssaye, then director of the Comédie-Française and a good friend, asking him to give Adèle the five hundred francs he had promised him, with a postscript: 'You are still not putting on my plays at all.'

His last years were embittered by constant wrangles with his publisher, Charpentier, to whom at his death Alfred owed more than ten thousand francs in advances which he had not worked off.

Yet he continued to live above his means. He was generous and charitable and would give the last five-franc piece in his pocket to a beggar.

Even his charity often had a poetic touch. One day at the seaside he saw a poor little girl in rags fast asleep in the sun, her head resting on a bale of straw. Alfred tiptoed up to the child and without waking her placed a gold coin between her lips; then tiptoed away, smiling at the thought of her amazed delight when on awaking she would discover this fairy-tale gift.

He was equally tender-hearted towards animals. Mlle Colin told him of a mongrel puppy that was about to be drowned in the Seine. Alfred immediately adopted it. Like so many mongrels Marzo turned out to possess exceptional intelligence; every evening he would carry three *sous* in a twist of paper to the newsvendor, returning to his master with *La Presse*. He lived until 1864, and when he died Adèle, who had since married, asked her husband to bury him near the Porte d'Auteuil, where a new quarter was then being built. The new street in which Marzo was lain to rest was afterwards called the Rue de Musset.

Alfred was given a perfectly hideous kitten as well, but could not bear to reject it. 'What can I do?' he remarked wryly, 'I did not choose them. They were given to me by chance and in those poor animals I respect and admire the phenomenon of life and nature's mysterious works.'

Mlle Colin often lectured him on his extravagance, but
rarely with any success. He was offered a very fine copy by
Carle Vanloo of the famous 'Concert' by Giorgione, in the
Louvre. He could not afford it, so he arranged to buy
it on the instalment plan. In spite of Adèle's protests he
proudly hung the picture in his dining-room, telling her:
'Always lay my place at table facing it and give me one course
less for dinner in future.'

There was one passion to which he had remained
faithful all his life, however often he deceived his mistresses.
This was his consuming love for the pictures of the Italian
Old Masters in the Louvre, which he had copied as a temporary
art student in his carefree youth. A year before his death he
had an irresistible desire to revisit them again—but at night,
and alone. This was in a way the most characteristically
romantic gesture of his whole life and one of the most dramatic.
He begged his friend Horace de Viel-Castel, the curator, to
arrange this for him and his request was granted. Viel-Castel
and his colleague Nieuwerkerke, director of the Louvre, and
Arsène Houssaye wished to accompany him. But Alfred begged
them to leave him in the gallery by himself. There was neither
gas nor electric lighting installed there at that period, so he
carried a hurricane lamp and in that sombre setting he spent
several hours in solitary contemplation of the magnificent
canvasses of Leonardo da Vinci, Raphael and their compatriots. He saw no ghosts except possibly those the pictures and
his memories evoked of his far-away visit to Italy. He knew
that this was the last time he would look at these masterpieces
and accepted the fact with resignation. Afterwards Viel-
Castel entertained Alfred and his other two friends to supper in
his apartment in the Museum.

In the following April Alfred received a command to dine
with Prince Napoléon at the Palais-Royal. He was weak and
ill and took so long to put on formal dress that he arrived too
late for dinner. But after it was over, Paul recorded:

He approached the Prince, joined in the conversation
and soon took the lead in it so that it became turn and
turn about serious, gay, and interesting . . . several people
who were there . . . told me that Alfred de Musset had

never seemed to them more charming and stimulating. It was his last outing. On his return home he took to his bed and was never able to leave it again.

His very last poem, written a few weeks before his death, expressed his conviction that he had little time to live:

L'heure de ma mort, depuis dix-huit mois,
De tous les côtés sonne à mes oreilles,
Depuis dix-huit mois d'ennuis et de veilles
Partout je la sens, partout je la vois.

Plus je me débats contre ma misère
Plus s'éveille en moi l'instinct du malheur:
Et dès que je veux faire un pas sur la terre,
Je sens tout à coup s'arrêter mon coeur.

Ma force à lutter s'use et se prodigue,
Jusqu'à mon repos, tout est un combat.
Et, comme un coursier, brisé de fatigue,
Mon courage éteint chancelle et s'abat.

For eighteen months I have heard the sound
Of the hour of my death ring in my ears,
I have felt and seen it all around
During eighteen months of sleepless fears.

The more my dread thoughts I would defeat,
The more forebodings my efforts foil.
I feel that my heart must cease to beat
When I try to stand on solid soil.

My strength in the struggle is wasted, torn,
And even sleep now from me flies.
Like a valiant steed, weary and worn,
My courage dims, dissolves, and dies.

Yet in spite of this intuition he had had for eighteen months that he was dying, he faced his death with courage and resignation.

Towards the end of April, alarmed at his condition, the faithful Adèle who was nursing him devotedly, sent for his brother. Paul arrived from Angers and stayed in Paris until the end. Alfred had for many years suffered from insomnia. During his sleepless nights when they had lived at home together, Paul had sometimes remained talking to him until dawn, frequently to argue with him or to calm the various manifestations of his anxiety neurosis. For Alfred had always worried himself into nervous exhaustion over everything, from financial stringency to an unkind criticism or a casual word of indifference from the woman with whom he was in love. Now, however, his attitude changed. He at last became a docile patient. Although he did not believe that he would recover, he tried to conceal his own view of his illness from Paul. He made plans for his next visit to Le Havre; took great interest in all Paul's activities and projects, asked after all those whom he loved, as if, Paul wrote, 'he wished to review his affections'. One of those of whom he spoke most tenderly was that dear Sister Marceline whom in imagination he could still see hovering smilingly around his bedside.

'What a lovely thing peace is,' he said on the evening of 1 May. 'It is a great mistake to be afraid of death, which is merely its highest form.'

Paul remained talking to him until one o'clock the next morning, when Alfred suddenly put his hand on his heart with an expression of surprise and concentration, but with no apparent alarm or fear. Paul asked him if he was suffering; he nodded negatively. A few minutes later he relaxed on his pillows.

'Sleep!' he sighed. 'At last I am going to sleep!'

He never woke again.

When next morning [Paul wrote] the first light of day came to shine on his features, they seemed to bear a superhuman beauty, as if all the great thoughts his genius had expressed so imperishably were making an aureole around his head.

5

As he had requested, the two humble little souvenirs given to him by Sister Marceline were placed in his coffin. He was buried in the cemetery of Père Lachaise, after a funeral service at Saint-Roch. There were no flowers on his bier, but only the cocked hat, sword and uniform of an 'Immortal'. A weeping willow was planted on his grave, a symbol of the long narrative poem *Le Saule*, which he had written when he was twenty.

At the time of his funeral a lady, dressed in black, was travelling in a railway carriage. A fellow passenger, seeing that she was in tears, asked kindly why she was weeping.

'Do you not know,' she answered, 'that Alfred de Musset is being buried to-day?'

The lady was Aimée d'Alton.

Bibliography

Note: There are a great number of French editions of the works of Alfred de Musset. For quotation and translation I have used the one-volume edition published by Charpentier, Paris, 1878.

The titles of the novel, poems, plays, short stories, etc., that I have quoted or discussed will be found in the Index.

MUSSET, Louis-Charles-Alfred de (see Index).

MUSSET, Paul de, *Biographie d'Alfred de Musset*, Paris, 1877; *Lui et Elle*, Paris, 1860.

SAND, George, *Lettres d'un Voyageur*, Paris, 1837; *Lélia* (second edition), Paris, 1839; *Un Hiver à Majorque*, Paris, 1842; *Histoire de ma Vie*, Paris, 1854; *Elle et Lui*, Paris, 1859; *Lettres à Alfred de Musset et à Sainte-Beuve*, Paris, 1897; *Correspondence* with Alfred de Musset, edited by Louis Evrard, Monaco, 1956.

ALLEM, Maurice, *Oeuvres complètes d'Alfred de Musset*, 3 vols., Paris, 1934-35-38.

D'ALMÉRAS, Henri, *La Vie parisienne sous le règne de Louis-Philippe*, Paris, 1911.

BARINE, Arvède, *Alfred de Musset*, Paris, 1893.

CABANÈS, Dr., *Les grands névropathes* (Vol. 2), Paris, 1931.

CHABRILLAN, Comtesse Lionel de, *Mémoires de Céleste Mogador*, Paris, 1854.

CHARPENTIER, John, *Alfred de Musset*, Paris, 1938.

COLIN, Adèle, *Dix ans chez Alfred de Musset*, Paris, 1899.

DONNAY, Maurice, *La Vie Amoureuse d'Alfred de Musset*, Paris, 1926.

HENRIOT, Émile, *Alfred de Musset*, Paris, 1928; *L'Enfant du Siècle*, Paris, 1953.

LOVENJOUL, Vicomte de Spoelberch de, *La Véritable Histoire de 'Elle et Lui'*, Paris, 1897.

MAURRAS, Charles, *Les Amants de Venise*, Paris, 1931.

MAUROIS, André, *Lélia*, English translation by Gerard Hopkins, London, 1954.

SÉCHÉ, Léon, *Études d'histoire romantique*, *Alfred de Musset*, 2 vols., Paris, 1907.

Index